# NOW PLAYING
## Learning Communication Through Film

### 2018 EDITION

**Darin Garard**
*Santa Barbara City College*

**Heidi Kirkman**
*Howard Community College*

**Mary Ann McHugh**

New York    Oxford
Oxford University Press

Oxford University Press is a department of the University of Oxford.
It furthers the University's objective of excellence in research,
scholarship, and education by publishing worldwide.

Oxford  New York
Auckland  Cape Town  Dar es Salaam  Hong Kong  Karachi
Kuala Lumpur  Madrid  Melbourne  Mexico City  Nairobi
New Delhi  Shanghai  Taipei  Toronto

With offices in
Argentina  Austria  Brazil  Chile  Czech Republic  France  Greece
Guatemala  Hungary  Italy  Japan Poland  Portugal  Singapore
South Korea  Switzerland  Thailand  Turkey  Ukraine  Vietnam

For titles covered by Section 112 of the US Higher Education
Opportunity Act, please visit www.oup.com/us/he for the
latest information about pricing and alternate formats.

Published by Oxford University Press
198 Madison Avenue, New York, New York 10016
http://www.oup.com

Oxford is a registered trademark of Oxford University Press

ISBN: 9780190917203

Printed by Sheridan Books, Inc., United States of America

# CONTENTS

## Section III: Full-Length Feature Films ..................................................... 73

## Section IV: Feature Film Websites ....................................................... 120

## Index by Communication Concepts ....................................................... 121

# INTRODUCTION

Communication is a human necessity—without it, we could scarcely coexist. Observing and analyzing communication patterns, interactions, and the many other intricacies of human contact is how we learn to project ourselves more effectively. Oftentimes it is difficult to evaluate our own communication processes in an objective manner—but watching people communicating in films can be an excellent way to identify and understand many aspects of communication. Closely watching others engaged in communication on film can help bring theories and concepts to life.

This manual contains sections on **Feature Film Scenes** and **Television Programs**—a variety of specific scenes that illustrate the good, the bad, and the ugly of human interaction, along with discussion questions for each scene. A third section, **Full-Length Feature Films,** provides examples of entire films that provide insights into human communication, with a detailed synopsis of the movie along with discussion questions to prompt critical thinking.

Looking at the various characters in these films struggle with communication can be liberating as well as enlightening—we can observe it from a distance and, without being too self-conscious, pick up on both the good and the bad habits that can lead us to become better communicators. Have fun learning!

# SECTION I
# FEATURE FILM SCENES

Each of the entries in this section is a "stand-alone" scene that illustrates communication concepts (with a strong focus on interpersonal communication). The scenes are listed in alphabetical order by film title; they are also arranged by category in the index at the end of the book. The time locations of the scenes are measured from the opening moment of the movie, just after the display of the film company (in other words, don't begin counting on your timer until all the previews on the video are finished).

**Film:** *10 Cloverfield Lane*
**Year:** 2016
**Central Concept:** Deception
**Related Concepts:** Self-Disclosure, Power
**Length and Location of Scene:** Approximately 5 minutes (00:43:00 minutes into 104-minute film)
**Opening Line:** "I know it's hard realizing they're all gone. The ones you love."
**Closing Line:** "You're doin' fine."

**Scene Description:** Michelle (Mary Elizabeth Winstead) is fleeing an unhappy relationship when, distraught and distracted, she crashes her car at night on a lonely stretch of road. After regaining consciousness, she finds herself banged up, alone, and chained to a pipe in what appears to be a bunker of some sort. The survivalist owner and builder of this subterranean complex, Howard (John Goodman), appears shortly after and explains that he rescued her not only from a car wreck but also from an attack of apocalyptic proportions, which may have been nuclear or chemical, human or alien. In any event, outside the protection of the underground shelter, the air is decidedly toxic, and the survivors are likely few in number.

Michelle, who remains both scared and skeptical, makes a subsequent bid to escape as soon as an opportunity presents itself. With Howard in hot pursuit, she desperately struggles to open the bunker door to get out, only to be confronted by a horribly disfigured woman on the other side equally desperate to get in—apparent confirmation of the survivalist's account of worldwide devastation. Following her failed escape, during which Howard stabs Michelle with a tranquilizing syringe, he makes an effort to set the record straight in this scene by revealing the true circumstances of her accident.

**Discussion Questions**
1. The film uses ambiguity to great effect, but, without giving away the surprise ending, it is safe to say that Howard is almost certainly lying about something in his account to Michelle. Research claims that interpersonal deception can often be detected through certain nonverbal microexpressions. What are some of these expressions? Consistent with this theory, does any of Howard's nonverbal communication suggest he is lying, or does he have black belts in both conspiracy theory and deception?

1

2.  What effect does Howard's self-disclosure appear to have on his relationship with Michelle?
3.  Howard uses a variety of methods to exercise interpersonal power and gain compliance. Describe these strategies.


**Film**: *50/50*
**Year**: 2011
**Central Concept**: Listening
**Related Concepts**: Social Support, Barriers to Effective Listening, Disconfirmation
**Length and Location of Scene 1**: Approximately 2 minutes (Chapter 2: 0:07:55–0:10:15)
**Opening Line**: "Hi."
**Closing Line**: "Now as I said, you should consider. . . ."
**Length and Location of Scene 2**: Approximately 1 minute (Chapter 3: 0:11:10–0:11:54)
**Opening Line**: "Oh Adam."
**Closing Line**: "Yeah, it will be okay. Alright?"
**Length and Location of Scene 3**: Approximately 2 minutes (Chapter 3: 0:11:55–0:13:50)
**Opening Line**: "I'm gonna throw up."
**Closing Line**: "I'm awake now."


**Scene Descriptions**: At 27 years of age, Adam (Joseph Gordon-Levitt) has a fairly normal life: he lives with his girlfriend Rachel (Bryce Dallas Howard), he works at a public radio station as a program writer, and his best friend Kyle (Seth Rogen) is often obnoxious. After a routine medical checkup, however, Adam is diagnosed with a rare form of spinal cancer and is given 50/50 odds of survival—hence the film's title. While Adam battles his cancer through chemotherapy and surgery, he experiences a number of different reactions from people once they learn about his condition.

Here are three scenes that illustrate different listening styles in response to Adam's diagnosis. Although each scene could stand alone, watching all three works very well in comparing and contrasting the characters' reactions to Adam's news. In the first scene, Adam's physician focuses on explaining the technical details of Adam's cancer and completely ignores the relational dimension of the message. In Scene 2, Rachel provides a supportive and comforting shoulder for Adam to lean on; watching the entire film, however, reveals Rachel's true colors. And in the third scene, when Kyle learns about the cancer, he reacts even more dramatically than Adam did; Kyle also provides advice that seems less than helpful. Taken together, these three scenes show how empathy and social support are necessary skills for competent communication. Indeed, at some point we each find ourselves in situations where others need our support.


**Discussion Questions**
1.  In Scene 1 Adam hears his diagnosis is cancer, but he immediately stops listening. Identify the causes of Adam's poor listening in this context. In this situation, is it possible for Adam to have been a better listener?
2.  Describe how Adam's physician broke the news to Adam in Scene 1. How could he have been more supportive and empathetic? Role play the situation in Scene 1 where you are the physician and someone else is Adam, and talk in a way that practices supportive communication.

3. Compare and contrast Rachel's responses in Scene 2 with Kyle's reactions in Scene 3. What does Rachel do that shows support? What does Kyle do? Are they both effective supportive listeners? Why or why not?
4. With regard to Rachel and Kyle's responses, are there inherent gender differences in how they provide social support to others? When you need support, do you seek out a male or a female? Why?

**Film:** *Almost Famous*
**Year:** 2000
**Central Concept:** Self-Disclosure
**Related Concepts:** Identity Management, Group Communication
**Approximate Scene Location:** 96 minutes into the 122-minute movie
**Approximate Scene Length:** 4 minutes
**Opening Line:** Brief shot of plane flying through storm (no dialogue)
**Closing Line:** "Thank God we're all alive. We're going to make it!" (To capture the facial expressions of the passengers after they realize they will survive, don't cut until the scene ends, about 10 seconds after the last line of dialogue.)

**Scene Description:** A 1970s rock band is on tour when its plane is caught in a violent storm. The prospect of imminent death moves several members of the group and its entourage to reveal facts and feelings they had previously kept to themselves. Some of the self-disclosing messages are positive; others are upsetting and disruptive. The scene offers a good foundation for exploring several dimensions of self-revelation: reasons for opening up, the conditions under which disclosure is likely to occur, and the risks and benefits of candor.
**Note: The scene contains language that may offend some viewers.**

**Discussion Questions**
1. Place the self-disclosures offered in this scene on a continuum, ranging from "appropriate under most conditions" to "inappropriate under most conditions." Describe the conditions under which the disclosures might be appropriate or inappropriate.
2. Which members of the group have been engaging in high levels of identity management with the others? What will happen to the management of their identities now that they've made these revelations?
3. Describe the following group communication concepts at work in this scene: ripple effect, conformity, openness, and boundaries.
4. Have you ever made a self-disclosure in a group of people that you later regretted? Discuss why you made the disclosure and how you managed your identity in later interactions with those people.

**Film:** *Arrival* (two scenes)
**Year:** 2016
**Central Concept:** Language
**Related Concepts:** Semiotics

**Length and Location of Scene 1**: Approximately 1 minute, 25 seconds (~ 0:16:00–0:17:25)
**Opening Line:** "Sorry, I couldn't hear what you were saying."
**Closing Line:** "This is why you're both here."
**Length and Location of Scene 2:** Approximately 4 minutes, 17 seconds (~ 0:36:10–0:40:27)
**Opening Line:** "What's that for?"
**Closing Line:** "Otherwise, this is gonna take 10 times as long."

**Scene Description:** In the first scene, linguistics professor Louise Banks (Amy Adams) is introduced to theoretical physicist Ian Donnelly (Jeremy Renner) on board a military flight to Montana, one of the sites around the globe where alien spacecrafts have just landed. U.S. Army officer Colonel Weber (Forest Whitaker) has recruited both researchers in the hope that they can establish communication with the extraterrestrials and learn the purpose of their arrival. The second scene features their second attempt to communicate with the "heptapods," an encounter in which Banks takes the lead with a linguistic approach she must subsequently justify to Weber.

**Discussion Questions**
1. How are the different approaches to the study of communication similar to the distinct perspectives of these researchers?
2. Are qualitative and quantitative research methods mutually exclusive, or can they be complementary?
3. "Language is the foundation of civilization. It is the glue that holds a people together. It is the first weapon drawn in a conflict." Donnelly quotes this assertion from the preface to Banks's book when they first meet, only to immediately dismiss it as "wrong." On what grounds does he reject Banks's argument, and whose position in this debate do you support?
4. How does this scene illustrate the basics of semiotic theory and the nature of the linguistic sign? Consider Banks's interaction with the heptapods and the "kangaroo" anecdote she uses to persuade Colonel Weber of the value of her method.

**Film**: *The Artist* (three scenes)
**Year**: 2011
**Central Concept**: Nonverbal Communication
**Related Concepts**: Relational Intimacy, Illustrators, Intercultural Competence
**Length and Location of Scene #1**: Approximately 3 minutes (00:18:30–0:21:42)
**Opening Line**: Inside the studio, they are about to start shooting a dance scene, and the director is instructing George Valentin about what to do.
**Closing Line**: After the final take, George walks off abruptly leaving Peppy perplexed on the dance floor.
**Length and Location of Scene 2**: Approximately 3 minutes (01:10:05–1:13:22)
**Opening Line**: George is about to strike a match to burn the film reels that cover the floor.
**Closing Line**: Title card reads: "I'll say one thing. He owes his life to that dog."
**Length and Location of Scene 3**: Approximately 2 minutes (1:19:20–1:21:25)

**Opening Line**: Actress Peppy is trying to persuade an unenthusiastic Zimmer to produce a new script featuring her and Valentin.

**Closing Line**: Elated Peppy blows Zimmer a big kiss.

**Scene Descriptions**: This 2013 silent film features the life and times of George Valentin (Jean Dujardin), a 1920s silent-film star rendered obsolete by the emergence of the "talkies." As his star continues to fall, that of Peppy Miller (Bérénice Bejo), the young ingénue whose career he helped launch, continues to rise. Despite the disparity in their ages and professional status over the years, they develop an artistic and romantic relationship that spans the film. In the first scene, George is thrilled to discover that Peppy has been cast as his partner in this dance sequence from a silent film in which he stars. Peppy, whom he knows only from a fleeting encounter, a brief episode of public flirtation that ended up front-page news, is still an unknown in Hollywood at this point. In the second scene, George, who has reached rock bottom some years later and set his house on fire in a drunken rampage, is rescued by the heroic efforts of his loyal canine companion, Jack (Uggie), a fearless Jack Russell Terrier. In the third scene, Peppy, who has been acting tirelessly and anonymously on George's behalf during his long fall from celebrity grace, makes a public stand on his behalf and leverages her star status to blackmail Al Zimmer (John Goodman), George's former producer, into accepting a script in which they costar.

**Discussion Questions**
1. In Scene 1, George and Peppy's relationship progresses with each of the five successive takes shot in a restaurant cabaret setting. Describe how nonverbal communication conveys their deepening relational intimacy. Then write dialogue for this scene in the form of the title cards used in silent films.
2. In Scene 2, Jack the Jack Russell terrier has trouble communicating his urgent message to the neighborhood police officer. When the cop points at him in frustration, for example, Jack flops over, assuming that he has been directed to play dead. Fortunately, the woman observing this interaction exhibits greater canine intercultural competence than the police officer and translates on Jack's behalf. Although animal communication is not a topic typically studied in communication courses, describe how Jack in this scene and dogs in general convey their feelings and desires nonverbally.
3. In Scene 3, a number of title cards supplement the nonverbal communication between Peppy and Zimmer. Would you have been able to get the gist of their conversation without this verbal script? Describe how the nonverbal communication in this scene conveys the dialogue, paying particular attention to the varied illustrators, nonverbals that accompany spoken words.

**Film**: *Boyhood*
**Year**: 2014
**Central Concept**: Listening
**Related Concept**: Relational Messages, Meta-communication
**Approximate Scene Location**: 34 minutes into the 165-minute movie
**Approximate Scene Length**: 3 minutes

**Opening Line:** "You guys ready for the big game?"
**Closing Line:** "Starting now."

**Scene Description:** In this scene, the dad (Ethan Hawke) has picked up Samantha (Lorelei Linklater) and Mason (Ellar Coltrane) for his weekend visit. He is taking them to a ballgame, and he tries to engage them in conversation. After getting only terse replies, he talks about how he'd like to see them communicate, and Mason counters with some thoughts of his own.

**Discussion Questions**
1. Do the kids appear to be listening in the initial conversation? What demonstrates that they are or are not listening?
2. What does the dad do to get their attention? Does it work?
3. Mason has a pretty mature response to his dad. Do you think they will be able to adjust how they communicate by discussing it?
4. When have you discussed how you communicate in a relationship? How did the conversation go? Were you able to initiate change?

**Film:** *Brooklyn* (two scenes)
**Year:** 2015
**Central Concept:** Relational Dialectics
**Related Concepts:** Intercultural Competence, Confirming and Disconfirming Messages
**Length and Location of Scene 1:** Approximately 5 minutes (00:45:00 into 117-minute film)
**Opening Line:** "Ready?"
**Closing Line:** "Then I'll wish I was back here talking to you."
**Length and Location of Scene 2:** Approximately 2.5 minutes (00:50:00 into film)
**Opening Line:** "Eilis, I'm sorry."
**Closing Line:** "Alright, I'm sorry."

**Scene Descriptions:** Seeking better opportunities than those available to young women in her small Irish town, Eilis (Saoirse Ronan), sponsored by an Irish priest (Hugh Gormley), leaves her close-knit family and relocates to Brooklyn circa 1950. After a trying and tearful first few months, the homesickness abates as Eilis starts creating a new life and ex-pat identity for herself. In addition to her retail job at a department store, she excels at night classes in bookkeeping at the local college. With her roommates at the boarding house, she attends community dances, where she meets Tony (Emory Cohen), whose self-professed attraction to Irish girls is exceeded only by his Italian-American charm. Romance blossoms, but not without missteps and miscommunication.

In the first of these two consecutive scenes, Eilis is introduced to Tony's family over dinner at his home. Subsequently, when they're alone together, Tony declares his love for Eilis, an intimate disclosure she fails to reciprocate. That night at the boarding house, an uncertain and confused Eilis broaches the subject of marriage with her housemate Sheila (Nora-Jane Noone). In the second scene that immediately follows, the couple maintains their routine of meeting up after her night class. On the walk home, the conversation that ensues is happily not the one an embarrassed Tony expected.

## Discussion Questions

1. In Scene 1, how does ethnicity affect the communication climate and inform the dinner conversation? What did Eilis do in advance of this important dinner to increase her intercultural competence? How do her hosts respond to these efforts?
2. In Scene 1, describe the confirming and disconfirming message(s) conveyed nonverbally by Tony and Eilis during dinner conversation.
3. In Scene 1, discuss Eilis and Sheila's conversation back at the boarding house in the context of relational dialectics.
4. In Scene 2, relational dialectics are again at the fore creating tensions that are at points almost palpable. Describe the different dialectics at play in Eilis and Tony's relationship at this stage.

**Film:** *Clueless*
**Year:** 1995
**Central Concept:** Language
**Related Concepts:** Culture, Communication Competence, Public Speaking
**Approximate Scene Location:** 30 seconds into the 97-minute film
**Approximate Scene Length:** 4 minutes
**Opening Line:** "Did I show you the lumped-out Jeep daddy got me?"
**Closing Line:** "If she doesn't do the assignment, I can't do mine."

**Scene Description:** Cher (Alicia Silverstone) and her friends live in their own "contempo-casual" culture and speak their own language (depicted throughout this scene with words such as "jeepin," "outie," and "buggin'"). Their linguistic code gives them a sense of shared identity and excludes those who are not in their group. Near the end of the scene, Cher uses her group's jargon in a public speaking context. Her speech is not successful though, demonstrating that language appropriate for an informal context is not appropriate for a formal one.

## Discussion Questions

1. Identify words/terms used by Cher and her friends that are unique to their culture. Which words/terms were not familiar to you?
2. Why do teenagers create new words or give old words new meanings?
3. Is it appropriate to use slang and jargon in public speeches?
4. Discuss this scene in terms of interpersonal, intercultural, and public speaking competence.

**Film**: *Crazy, Stupid, Love*
**Year**: 2011
**Central Concept**: Listening
**Related Concepts**: Identity Management, Scripts, Self-Disclosure, Expectancy Violations
**Length and Location of Scene**: Approximately 3 minutes (Chapter 5: 0:41:32–0:44:02)
**Opening Line**: "Just no talking about your kids, your job."
**Closing Line**: "That's what you picked up from what I just said?"

**Scene Description**: Cal Weaver (Steve Carell) is your stereotypical middle-aged man: married to his wife for 20-plus years, with three children, a large house, and a steady job. When his wife, Emily (Julianne Moore), unexpectedly reveals that she cheated on him and wants a divorce, Cal's life is turned upside down and inside out. Although he capitulates and moves into an apartment, it's clear that Cal misses his relationship with Emily. To combat his depression and loneliness, Cal begins frequenting the local bar scene. There, he meets Jacob (Ryan Gosling), a self-proclaimed savant when it comes to talking with, and taking home, women. Jacob takes pity on Cal, and vows to teach him "the art of the pick-up."

Prior to this scene Cal has already observed how Jacob interacts with women, successfully administering one pick-up line after another. Now, Jacob convinces Cal that he is ready to "fly solo" and secure a date on his own. Jacob singles out Kate (Marisa Tomei), introductions are made, and the initial interaction ensues. Observe how Cal navigates this uncharted territory, as his identity management and self-disclosure are unique, to put it mildly. And pay close attention to Kate as well. After listening to Cal, is she really going to fall for his advances?

**Discussion Questions**
1. Which type of faulty or ineffective listening behavior is Kate guilty of as she listens to Cal? In addition, what are the possible reasons why Kate engages in this type of ineffective listening?
2. Identify a time in your life when you were the one who demonstrated ineffective listening. What effect did your faulty listening have on the conversation? How can you work toward reducing your ineffective listening?
3. In the scene, Cal comments on several things that he "was supposed to say." In other words, Cal was encouraged to use a conversational script, and in particular a dating script. How common are scripts during initial interactions, especially in the dating context? Do you notice these scripts, and if so, what are your reactions when you hear them? Do they work?
4. Looking at this scene from a self-disclosure perspective, and particularly the social penetration model, how would you describe the depth and breadth of information Cal volunteered? Did he follow the typical rules for effective self-disclosure? Explain.
5. How would the expectancy violation model explain the outcome of their conversation? Use the terms *expectancies, violation valence*, and *communicator reward valence* in your answer.

**Film**: *Creed* (4 scenes)
**Year**: 2015
**Central Concept**: Listening
**Related Concepts**: Social Support, Self-disclosure, Noise, Content and Relational Messages, Relational Stages
**Length and Location of Scene 1**: Approximately 2 minutes (00:13:30 into 133-minute film)
**Opening Line**: "Hey, how ya doin'?"
**Closing Line**: "Listen, you want to be in somebody's ring, you don't have to call me."
**Length and Location of Scene 2**: Approximately 2 minutes (00:52:00 into film)

**Opening Line**: "Lighten it up."
**Closing Line**: "Ah, you cheated."
**Length and Location of Scene 3**: Approximately 2 minutes (1:04:30 into film)
**Opening Line**: "What's up?"
**Closing Line**: "Just to get on my nerves."
**Length and Location of Scene 4**: Approximately 2 minutes (1:20:52 into film)
**Opening Line**: "This shit for real?"
**Closing Line**: "Why did you say that?"

**Scene Descriptions:** *Creed*, the critically acclaimed seventh installment in the remarkably enduring *Rocky* franchise, introduces us to Adonis or Donnie (Michael B. Jordan), the son of Apollo Creed from an extramarital affair. After the death of his biological mother, Creed's wife, Mary Anne (Phylicia Rashad), adopts Donnie and reveals the secret of his paternity. Donnie never knew his dad, but aptly in Rocky Balboa (Sylvester Stallone), he finds both a trainer and a father figure.

In *Creed*, a round of verbal sparring often follows a round of physical fighting, making this sports-drama a film about much more than boxing. An early interaction, immediately preceding the first scene in this group of four, establishes Donnie as listening-challenged: "I try to tell you things. You don't want to listen. You want to do things the hard way." The young protagonist is not alone in his tendency to hear but not listen. Various obstacles to effective listening shape the following scenes for all the central characters. In the first, Donnie shares the unwelcome news with Mary Anne that he has quit his job in the financial sector to follow in his father's pugilist footsteps. In the second, Donnie lets emotion deafen him to Rocky's instructions when sparring with a new partner. In the third, Donnie's new girlfriend, Bianca (Tessa Thompson), discovers that he has failed to disclose significant information about himself to her. And in the fourth, Rocky responds poorly when confronted about his potentially lethal cancer diagnosis.

**Discussion Questions**
1. In Scene 1, how does Mary Anne respond to the shocking, yet not entirely unexpected, news from Donnie? Given both the immediate circumstances and her history with her husband, Apollo, could Mary Anne have reasonably been expected to be a better listener? What could Donnie have done to encourage more effective listening?
2. In Scene 2, Rocky delivers one of the best lines in the movie—quote-worthy and pithy advice about listening. What does he say? Describe an experience from your professional or personal life where this counsel would have been wise to apply.
3. In Scene 3, Bianca makes a startling discovery. What does she learn, and is her reaction to this news justified? Why is self-disclosure critical to her? Consider both gender and the stage of her romantic relationship with Donnie in your response. Compare the content and relational messages at the end of this scene.
4. In Scene 4, it is Rocky who neglects to share significant information, a failure he compounds by responding to Donnie's efforts to provide social support with disconfirming messages. Rocky acknowledges his mistakes only after Donnie storms out of the locker room. What might both listeners have done differently? Describe the types of noise that affected their ability to listen and to offer and accept social support.

**Film:** *Dallas Buyers Club*
**Year:** 2013
**Central Concept:** Communication Climate
**Related Concepts:** Perception, Language, Content and Relational Messages, Gender and Sex Roles
**Length and Location of Scene 1**: 2 minutes, 30 seconds (exact location 0:31:04–0:34:34)
**Opening Line:** "My name is Rayon."
**Closing Line:** "Anyone who plays cards like you ain't got five grand anyhow."

**Scene Description:** In this scene, Ron Woodroof (Matthew McConaughey) first meets the transgendered Rayon (Jared Leto) who is also in the hospital from AIDS-related illness. Although Ron is uncomfortable with Rayon's transgender identity, the two start playing cards, with Rayon taking Ron's money. Rayon reveals that he's being paid to test AZT for a friend.

**Discussion Questions (Scene 1)**
1. What perceptual tendencies may have led to troublesome communication in this scene?
2. Identify as many nonverbal cues as you can (e.g., haptics, proxemics) that are played out in the scene and discuss their relationship to the communication climate.
3. Compare the characters' content messages with their relational messages. Do their relational messages support the content of what they say, or do they contradict it?
4. What role did impression management play in how Rayon and Ron communicated with each other?
5. Think about when your perceptions were distorted about someone you learned to care about. Identify what influenced those inaccurate perceptions? Were they distorted perceptions about yourself? How have you learned to be more empathic to others?

**Length and Location of Scene 2:** 3 minutes (exact location 1:25:25–1:28:25)
**Opening Line:** "I met someone who's been very kind to me."
**Closing Line:** "Thank you."

**Scene Description:** The scene begins with Rayon (Jared Leto) dressed in masculine clothing asking his father for money to help keep the Dallas Buyers Club afloat. A handshake and a hug at the end symbolize Ron Woodroof's (Matthew McConaughey) transformation from a homophobic bigot to a less judgmental version of his former self.

**Discussion Questions (Scene 2):**
1. Compare Rayon's presenting self in the first scene versus the second scene. What about Rayon's identity management has changed? Use the terms manner, appearance, and setting in your answer.
2. Looking at both of these scenes together, we find that social expectations and our relationships with others have a powerful influence on how we communicate. What does this observation tell you about sex and gender roles?

3. Analyze how Ron and Rayon communicate in this scene (verbally and nonverbally) that demonstrates an improvement in their relationship.
4. Recall a relationship with someone that changed your perceptions, attitudes, and communication positively. Identify what changed.
5. Consider your own experiences managing your identity, gendered or otherwise. Think of a particular moment when you struggled to hide your true self from someone else. Analyze why you were cautious in revealing your identity. Was it fear of being judged? Was it the need to save face, either yours or someone else's? Please explain.

**Film:** *Dead Man Walking*
**Year:** 1996
**Central Concept:** Perception (Stereotyping and Prejudice)
**Related Concepts:** Communication Climate, Listening, Language
**Approximate Scene Location:** 40 minutes into the 120-minute film
**Approximate Scene Length:** 3 minutes
**Opening Line:** "Rain, rain, rain . . . that's a bad sign." (in the middle of a prison cell discussion)
**Closing Line:** "Can we talk about something else?"

**Scene Description:** This scene is an interpersonal communication tour de force. Helen Prejean (Susan Sarandon) is a nun who befriends death-row prisoner Matthew Poncelet (Sean Penn) prior to his execution. She confronts Poncelet about his prejudices regarding African Americans. Poncelet's perceptions and language are filled with stereotypes and generalizations about "niggers" and "coloreds." Prejean's questions and responses require him to think (which he doesn't seem to want to do) about inaccuracies in his generalizations. Some of her comments are loaded and get defensive reactions; most are reflective and allow Poncelet to hear his prejudices in another voice. When Prejean's probing digs too deep (she gets him to realize "it's lazy people you don't like," not blacks), Poncelet asks Prejean to change the subject—which she agrees to do. This scene is worthy of line-by-line analysis.

**Discussion Questions**
1. What factors influenced Poncelet's perceptions, prejudices, and stereotypes?
2. What listening skills does Prejean use to draw information from Poncelet? How do these skills get/keep Poncelet talking and thinking?
3. What questions/statements by Prejean prompt a defensive response from Poncelet?
4. Discuss the use of responsible and irresponsible language in the scene and its relationship to communication climate.

**Film**: *The Descendants*
**Year**: 2011
**Central Concept**: Self-Disclosure
**Related Concepts**: Privacy, Conflict, Relational Dialectics
**Length and Location of Scene**: Approximately 5 minutes (Chapter 10: 0:29:35–0:34:15)
**Opening Line**: "Watch your sister."
**Closing Line**: "I guess it doesn't matter."

**Scene Description**: In his own words, Matt King (George Clooney) is "the back-up parent," while his wife Elizabeth (Patricia Hastie) is the one who manages the relationships in their family and takes care of their two daughters. Sadly, Elizabeth was recently involved in a boating accident, and now she lies in a hospital bed in a coma. Because of the accident, Matt is forced to reexamine his life: his workaholic nature, the pending sale of his family's expansive land trust, and what it means to be a loving husband and father. When her doctor diagnoses Elizabeth's condition as terminal, Matt suddenly realizes that he alone will have to break the news to their family members and friends. And when Matt learns that Elizabeth was having an affair before the accident, he's not quite sure what to think.

In this scene, Matt's older daughter Alexandra (Shailene Woodley) has just told him about the affair—which is why she had been so angry with her mother. Stupefied, Matt runs over to the home of Elizabeth's friend, Kai (Mary Birdsong) and her husband Mark (Rub Huebel). There, Matt confronts Kai and Mark about their knowledge of the affair. To label this moment as emotionally awkward would be an understatement. Watch how the characters manage their disclosure of this private information, and their decisions to conceal or reveal. If you were in this situation, what would you do?

**Note: Consider pausing the scene about halfway through, at the 0:32:42 mark, and discuss the first two discussion questions that follow. Then watch the remainder of the scene to answer Questions 3 and 4.**

**Discussion Questions**
1. Place yourself in Kai and Mark's position, one at a time. How would you have handled knowing this private information (the affair) if you were Kai? Would you have disclosed this information to Matt? What if you were Mark? Does gender make a difference?
2. Which dialectical tensions are demonstrated in this scene? How does each of the characters choose to manage these dialectics? Hint: All three characters make different choices.
3. Why did Matt suddenly reveal to Kai that his wife, Elizabeth, is going to die? Was Matt's disclosure appropriate? Whose disclosure was more justified: Kai's decision to keep the affair a secret or Matt's decision to disclose Elizabeth's diagnosis at this moment? Please explain your reasoning.
4. What are some criteria or questions that you ask of yourself when you are deciding whether to reveal private information to someone else? Please make a list of these criteria and compare them with those of another classmate. Any similarities? Differences?

**Film**: *Election*
**Year**: 1999
**Central Concept**: Persuasion
**Related Concept**: Public Speaking
**Approximate Scene Location**: 36 minutes into the 103-minute film
**Approximate Scene Length**: 5 minutes
**Opening Line**: "We'll move on now to the presidential race."
**Closing Line**: "Don't vote at all!"

**Scene Description**: Three candidates are running for student government president at Carver High School: Tracy (Reese Witherspoon), Paul (Chris Klein), and Tammy (Jessica Campbell). Each is required to give a brief speech at a student assembly. Tracy's presentation is memorized, well constructed, and delivered with precision and flair (and a dose of overconfidence, which generates crude catcalls from students who think she is stuck up). Paul, a popular athlete, reads his speech directly from his notecards. While his content is solid, he has little or no eye contact, facial expression, or vocal variety—and the students don't know how to respond (they are prompted to applaud by a teacher). Tammy, Paul's sister, thinks that student government is a joke; she is running for election to spite her brother and his girlfriend. She speaks extemporaneously and with passion about the "pathetic" election process and encourages people to either vote for her or not vote at all. She gets a rousing response.

**Discussion Questions:**
1. Identify the strengths and weaknesses of each of the candidates' speeches.
2. Evaluate the persuasive appeals of each candidate in terms of logos, pathos, and ethos.
3. Which candidate would get your vote—and why?

**Film:** *The Fits* (two scenes)
**Year:** 2015
**Central Concept:** Group Conformity
**Related Concepts:** In-group–Out-group Bias, Gender
**Length and Location of Scene 1:** Approximately 1 minute (00:28:16 into film)
**Opening Line:** "How's your sister?"
**Closing Line:** Gasping and gagging.
**Length and Location of Scene 2:** Approximately 4:30 minutes (00:59:00 into film)
**Opening Line:** "Where are your earrings?"
**Closing Line:** "Keep workin'."

**Scene Description:** *The Fits* follows the social transition and development of Toni (Royalty Hightower), an 11-year-old tomboy whom we first meet training rigorously with her older brother at the local boxing gym. When she joins the Lionesses, a girls' dance group that practices in another gym at the same recreation center, she moves from a masculine space to a feminine one, making two new girlfriends in the process, Beezy (Alexis Neblett) and Maia (Lauren Gibsen). Meanwhile, the Lionesses have begun succumbing one by one to "the fits," a source of consternation for Toni, particularly when Maia ostensibly suffers a seizure shortly after confessing to Toni her desire for one. In the first scene, we see the team react to Karisma's (Inayah Rodgers) convulsions, the second team captain to have an episode. In the next scene, Toni watches through the office window as Beezy begins to have a seizure during her interview about this phenomenon, after which the three friends wait together outside for Beezy's ride. Then Toni is left alone to contemplate this series of bizarre events as the older dancers, chatting across the hall, all eagerly share the details of their episodes.

## Discussion Questions

1.  In Scene 1, dancers record the team captain's seizure on their phones as it is happening. In similar circumstances, would you film this episode? With whom would you share it? Would you post this on social media? When does such behavior violate the right to privacy of the person being filmed?
2.  In Scene 2, Toni and Beezy remain close friends before Beezy enters the exclusive "fits" club. How do they convey their friendship verbally and nonverbally outside the office at the rec center?
3.  In Scene 2, describe how the communication climate among the three friends changes after both Beezy and Maia have exhibited a fit. Why do you think this occurs? Consider in-group–out-group bias, and describe the role group conformity might play in the team's seizure epidemic.
4.  In Scene 2, the older team members in the hallway are happily comparing the details of their seizure experiences, much like Beezy and Maia. Research indicates that a feminine style of communication features the "matching" of experiences. In your experience, do people with a feminine style of communication bond through discussion of similar experiences? How do people with a masculine style of communication achieve closeness?
5.  What do you think occurs for Toni after this scene? Does she too succumb to "the fits"?

**Film**: *Friends with Benefits*
**Year**: 2011
**Central Concept**: Intimacy
**Related Concepts**: Friends with Benefits Relationships, Social Exchange Theory, Relationship Rules, Relational Dialectics
**Length and Location of Scene**: Approximately 5 minutes (Chapter 5: 0:24:20–0:29:20)
**Opening Line**: "I can't do this anymore."
**Closing Line**: "Swear."

**Scene Description**: Dylan (Justin Timberlake) is an art director at a small Internet company in California, and Jamie (Mila Kunis) is a corporate head hunter based out of New York City. When Jamie successfully recruits Dylan to be the new art design coordinator for *GQ* magazine in New York, she is the only person he knows in the entire city. They soon become platonic friends, as both of them recently ended an intimate relationship, and emotional commitment is currently at the bottom of their respective lists. However, their mutual need for physical intimacy is still rather high. Dylan and Jamie decide to try to maintain their relationship as friends, but with sexual benefits. Can two friends keep their relationship strictly physical—just sex—without any emotional intimacy?

In this scene, Jamie and Dylan are spending time together, as platonic friends, watching romantic movies. As they talk about their past romantic relationships, both of them realize that right now they want a sexual relationship without emotions or commitment. Together they make a pact and decide to give the "friends-with-benefits relationship" a try. Considering what you have learned about the definitions of intimacy and commitment, do Jamie and Dylan have a "real" interpersonal relationship?

## Discussion Questions

1. Use social exchange theory to describe the potential costs and rewards of a friends-with-benefits relationship. Are their possible differences between males' and females' cost/reward analysis of friends-with-benefits relationships?
2. How might male and female intimacy styles affect this type of relationship? Explain.
3. Based on your knowledge of friends-with-benefits relationships, create a list of "rules" that could be used to maintain this type of relationship. How do these maintenance rules differ from platonic cross-sex friendships? From romantic relationships?
4. Which relational dialectics would be most prominent in a friends-with-benefits relationship? How would partners in this type of relationship manage these dialectics?

**Film:** *Get Out* (three scenes)
**Year:** 2017
**Central Concept:** Uncertainty Reduction, Race
**Related Concepts:** Emotions, Nonverbal Communication
**Length and Location of Scene 1**: Approximately 1 minute 40 seconds (~ 0:6:50–0:08:30)
**Opening Line:** "How is it going over there?"
**Closing Line:** "Yeah, yeah, good."
**Length and Location of Scene 2:** Approximately 4 minutes (~ 0:17:50–0:21:50)
**Opening Line:** "Georgina, this is Chris. This is Rose's boyfriend."
**Closing Line:** "Yes, I think I will."
**Length and Location of Scene 3:** Approximately 4 minutes, 17 seconds (~ 0:42:10–0:43:50)
**Opening Line:** "Oh man, it begins. Are you ready for this?"
**Closing Line:** "But now the pendulum has swung back. Black is in fashion."

**Scene Description:** Chris (Daniel Kaluuya), a talented young, black photographer, takes a trip with Rose (Allison Williams), his white girlfriend, to her family's country home. Chris has concerns about meeting her parents (Catherine Keener and Bradley Whitford) for the first time, especially once Rose reveals that she has not told them he is black. When they arrive, Chris doesn't know what to make of her seemingly liberal family who employ zombie-like black staff. In the third scene, during the Armitages' annual house party, the odd behavior of the guests upon meeting him only serves to increase his anxiety.

## Discussion Questions

1. Uncertainty reduction theory asserts that people need to reduce uncertainty about others by gaining information about them. Describe the passive, active, and interactive strategies that Chris uses in the first two scenes to learn about the Armitage family.
2. Charles Berger and Richard Calabrese posited seven axioms of uncertainty reduction theory. What are these axioms, and how are they illustrated in the first two scenes as Chris develops a relationship with Rose's parents?
3. Describe how Chris's emotions change across these three scenes. How does he convey these emotions?
4. Describe the nature of the racially-charged verbal and nonverbal communication of guests at the Armitages' party when they meet Chris.

**Film:** *The Grand Budapest Hotel*
**Year:** 2014
**Central Concept:** Perception
**Related Concepts:** Emotional Expression, Relational Messages, Listening
**Approximate Scene Location:** 59 minutes into the 99-minute movie
**Approximate Scene Length:** 4 minutes
**Opening Line:** "Good evening."
**Closing Line:** "I insist you finish later."

**Scene Description:** Gustave (Ralph Fiennes) is the very well-known concierge at the Grand Budapest Hotel. He has been framed for the murder of a wealthy patroness, and has been put in jail. His protégé (and the lobby boy at the Grand Budapest), Mr. Moustafa (F. Murray Abraham), has smuggled tools into the jail so that Gustave and a few other convicts can escape. This scene begins with Gustave climbing out of the sewer and meeting up with Moustafa, and then questioning Moustafa's escape plans.

**Discussion Questions**
1. What are Gustave's expectations of a great escape from jail? How do they compare to the reality of his situation?
2. Why does Gustave lash out at Moustafa? How does Moustafa react?
3. How do the two men differ in terms of their emotional expression?
4. What expectations have you had in a situation that influenced how you perceived the situation? How did you communicate in that situation? What was the outcome?

**Film:** *The Great Gatsby*
**Year:** 2013
**Central Concept:** Nonverbal Communication
**Related Concepts:** Identity Management, Relational Messages
**Approximate Scene Location:** 52 minutes into the 143-minute movie
**Approximate Scene Length:** 4 minutes
**Opening Line:** "Is there anything you need?"
**Closing Line:** "I'm certainly glad to see you as well."

**Scene Description:** Nick Carraway (Tobey Maguire) moves into a cottage next door to the eccentric millionaire Jay Gatsby (Leonardo DiCaprio). He discovers that Gatsby knew and was in love with his cousin Daisy five years previously. Gatsby asks Nick to invite Daisy to tea so Gatsby can see her again. After sending gardeners over to Nick's cottage to clean up the grounds, Gatsby arrives for tea with an extensive menu of food and a proliferation of flowers. This scene begins with Gatsby nervously waiting for Daisy to arrive and goes through their first interaction in five years.

## Discussion Questions

1. Identify the range of identities Gatsby displays. How is he using his nonverbals to present those identities?
2. Though few words are exchanged between Gatsby and Daisy, it seems much more is communicated. What relational messages are conveyed? How are they conveyed?
3. What are the functions of the nonverbal in this scene?
4. How do you create your identities? What nonverbals do you use to create an identity at school? At work? On a date?

**Film**: *The Help*
**Year**: 2011
**Central Concept**: Listening
**Related Concepts**: Supportive Listening, Confirmation, Self-Fulfilling Prophecy
**Length and Location of Scene**: Approximately 3 minutes (Chapter 3: 0:23:15–0:26:00)
**Opening Line**: "What you doing hiding out here, girl?"
**Closing Line**: "Come on go home with me until the dance is over. Come on."

**Scene Description**: Set in civil rights-torn Jackson, Mississippi, in the 1960s, *The Help* is a fictional story about Skeeter Phelan (Emma Stone). Always the rebellious one in her family, Skeeter eschews the socialite lifestyle of her friends. After graduating from Ole Miss, she seeks out and earns a job as a journalist. However, writing for the local paper about housekeeping tips is not what Skeeter had in mind. Instead, she hatches the idea of writing a book about the stories of black housekeepers—known as "the help"—who work for well-to-do white families in Jackson. Recruiting the housekeepers turns out to be a challenge, but Skeeter eventually finishes her book. And when it hits the store shelves, it creates quite the scandal in Jackson. On the surface, *The Help* is about people overcoming prejudice and racism in their community. But it's also about listening to people tell their stories. And, to paraphrase a line from the film, it's about confirming that all of us are "kind, smart, and important."

Immediately before this scene, Skeeter has learned that her mother, Charlotte (Allison Janney), recently fired the family's longtime housekeeper, Constantine (Cicely Tyson). Angry and bitter, Skeeter storms out of the house and marches straight toward a sitting bench on the family property. As she gets closer to the bench, Skeeter relives a teenage moment when Constantine comforted her. Watch how Constantine's supportive listening style confirms Skeeter's identity, and sets her back on a path of positive self-regard.
**Note: There are several additional scenes of confirmation in the film, particularly when another housekeeper (Aibileen, played by Viola Davis) speaks to the children she watches over.**

## Discussion Questions

1. Describe how Constantine uses supportive listening with Skeeter. Which particular types of supportive responses does Constantine use? Is a combination of responses always effective? Please explain.
2. How does Constantine create a self-fulfilling prophecy for Skeeter? Do you believe Skeeter will internalize this self-fulfilling prophecy? Why or why not?

3. Recall a moment in your life when someone was a supportive listener for you. Specifically, what did the other person say and do to make you feel supported? Please describe in detail.
4. Do you consider yourself to be a good listener? What specific goals can you set for yourself to be a more supportive listener of others? Please make a list of these goals now, and in one week revisit the list. Were you successful in improving your listening skills?

**Film**: *Her*
**Year**: 2013
**Central Concept**: Computer-Mediated Communication/Technology/Social Media
**Related Concepts**: Self-Disclosure, Identity Management
**Length and Location of Scene 1**: Approximately 2 minutes and 20 seconds (*Interplay* YouTube channel; exact location 0:60:48–0:63:08)
**Opening Line**: "I even made a new friend."
**Closing Line**: "It's kind of like a form of socially acceptable insanity."

**Scene Description**: In the not-too-distant future, Theodore Twombly (Joaquin Phoenix) lives alone in a high-rise apartment, wounded on the heels of a failed marriage. He spends his days in a cubicle at BeautifulHandwrittenLetters.com writing warm, sensitive messages for other people.

Theodore's life changes when he buys an artificially intelligent operating system who calls herself Samantha (voiced by the disembodied Scarlett Johansson). With a beguiling personality and insights more keen than those of most humans, Samantha draws Theodore out of his self-imposed shell and helps him find joy in everyday life. Before long they grow to love one another. As in every relationship, the couple struggles to meet their differing needs.

Unlike most flesh-and-blood partners, Theodore and Samantha build their relationship entirely on speech. Their only tools are their words and voices. That's enough to achieve a level of intimacy most couples would relish.

It's easy to view this romance as a warning about the dangers of our digital era. Whether or not technology can indeed satisfy our interpersonal needs, the movie *Her* demonstrates that emotional connection is what humans crave, and that they'll go to great lengths to find it.

In this scene, Theodore's friend Amy (Amy Adams) confides in him that she has struck up a friendship with an operating system. In turn, he confesses that he is dating Samantha, and may be falling in love with her.
**Note: The clip on the YouTube channel has been edited to exclude the characters' discussion of sex. Instructors can show the full clip using the times indicated above.**

### Discussion Questions
1.  Identify the types of technologies you utilize to initiate or maintain relationships. In what ways might your relationships with these technologies themselves be considered intimate?
2.  Is mediated communication sometimes preferable to face-to-face interaction? When is this the case, and how so?
3.  Consider the self-disclosures in this scene. How are the characters' revelations risky or beneficial?
4.  Have you ever made a self-disclosure you were reluctant to make? How did you manage your identity in light of it?

**Film:** *Inside Out*
**Year:** 2015
**Central Concept:** Intrapersonal Communication
**Related Concepts:** Emotions, Interpersonal Communication, Conflict, Disconfirming Messages, Gendered Communication, Stereotypes
**Length and Location of Scene:** Approximately 3.5 minutes (00:26:45 into 95-minute film)
**Opening Line:** "So as it turns out the green trash can is not for recycling, it's for greens like compost and eggshells."
**Closing Line:** Riley slams the door to her room.

**Scene Description:** When Riley's family moves from Minnesota to San Francisco, her exterior world becomes a foreign and seemingly hostile place, and her interior world a confused and decidedly unhappy one in response. The action in this acclaimed Pixar dramedy occurs largely inside the mind of an 11-year-old protagonist as her personified central emotions—joy, sadness, disgust, anger, fear—attempt to guide her adjustment to a new home, school, and city. All this upheaval shakes Riley's emotional apparatus to its very core, and conflict naturally ensues among well-intentioned but frequently misguided emotions that end up vying for control of her psychological headquarters during this crisis period.

This scene follows a humiliating first day at her new school that featured the teacher asking Riley to introduce herself, an exercise in impromptu public speaking that ended in tears. Later, at the dinner table, Riley's mom is not sure why her characteristically happy daughter is not herself. Here we see the psychological drama unfold in the emotional headquarters of Riley and both parents in a compelling illustration of the relationship between intrapersonal and interpersonal communication and conflict.

### Discussion Questions
1.  Describe how the intrapersonal communication of these characters influenced their interpersonal communication. In what ways did their intrapersonal states affect the communication climate and contribute to the ensuing interpersonal conflict?
2.  Identify the disconfirming messages exchanged in this escalatory spiral, and describe what steps might have been taken to curtail it.

3. This scene plays with gendered communication stereotypes for comic effect. Describe how the emotional headquarters for Riley's mom and dad enact certain stereotypes. How does this gendered behavior work to resolve or exacerbate interpersonal conflict? How accurate in your experience is this depiction of gendered communication?

**Film**: *The Invention of Lying*
**Year**: 2009
**Central Concept**: Self-Disclosure
**Related Concepts**: Honesty, Uncertainty Reduction, Identity Management, Saving Face
**Approximate Scene Location:** 4 minutes into the 99-minute film
**Approximate Scene Length**: 3 minutes
**Opening Line**: "This is not as nice as I remember it."
**Closing Line**: "How is your mom? Alright? Great!"

**Scene Description**: *The Invention of Lying* is a fictional tale about a world where no one can tell a lie, not even a fib or a white lie—except one man. Mark Bellison (Ricky Gervais) discovers his unique gift and sets out to solve all of the world's problems, become rich and famous, and win the heart of the woman he loves. Predictably, Mark's plans do not always turn out the way he envisioned them. Perhaps the film would be more aptly titled *Too Much Self-Disclosure*, since the storyline really isn't so much about lying. Instead, it's more about the inability to refrain from verbalizing your every thought. The characters say whatever pops into their heads, no matter the context, and apparently without any negative outcomes—indeed a fictional tale. In this scene, Mark is on a date with Anna McDoogles (Jennifer Garner). It is a typical first-date scenario for both characters, complete with feelings of uncertainty and anxiety about each other. Well, it's typical except for one small detail: they cannot control their self-disclosure. Pay special attention to the topics that are discussed, along with their atypical answers. In a world where honesty isn't simply the best policy—it's the only policy—a little self-disclosure can go a very long way.

**Discussion Questions**
1. Using the terms *depth*, *breadth*, and *reciprocity of self-disclosure*, how is their first date typical of most first dates? How is it different from most first dates?
2. Consider your own past experiences on first dates. What topics do you typically discuss? Are these topics goal-oriented (e.g., to reduce uncertainty, to secure a second date)? In what ways?
3. Compare and contrast the characters' public and private selves. How are they managing their identity through communication?
4. Describe a situation in which you were aware of your different selves, and you felt the need to manage your identity. Were you successful?
5. Is honesty always the best policy? Describe a situation in which saving someone's face, without being completely honest, was the best choice—the choice of a competent communicator.

**Film**: *Invictus*
**Year**: 2009
**Central Concept**: Persuasive Speaking
**Related Concepts**: Credibility, Audience Analysis, Leadership and Power
**Approximate Scene Location:** 27 minutes into the 134-minute film
**Approximate Scene Length**: 8 minutes
**Opening Line**: "And now for the next item on our agenda."
**Closing Line**: "A luxury. We only needed one more yes than no."

**Scene Description**: *Invictus* is the real-life story about then South African President Nelson Mandela and his plan to use rugby to unite his country following the demise of apartheid. Set in 1994–1995, newly elected President Mandela (played by Morgan Freeman) is struggling to move his nation forward, both politically and economically, in the eyes of the world. While attending a rugby match of the Springboks, the country's national rugby team, Mandela notices that blacks actually cheer against their home team—for them a longstanding symbol of racism and hatred—while Afrikaners (whites) root for the Springboks. Knowing that South Africa will host the Rugby World Cup in one year, Mandela enlists the aid of the Springboks' captain to promote the sport as a symbol of unity and nationalism instead of hatred and violence. In this scene, Mandela must persuade South Africa's National Sports Council (the governing body in charge of the country's sports) not to change the Springboks team's name and colors. The National Sports Council, like most of the country's black citizens, views the Springboks as a symbol of apartheid. Learning that the Council has voted to dismantle the Springboks, Mandela rushes to their meeting in an attempt to persuade them otherwise. Facing a hostile audience, Mandela uses his credibility and audience analysis to successfully, by a narrow margin, bring the Council around to his viewpoint.

**Discussion Questions**
1. Using the terms propositions, outcomes, and directness, identify the type of persuasive speech Mandela gives.
2. How does Mandela adapt to his audience (the National Sports Council)? What strategies does he use to appeal to this target audience?
3. Recall a time when you gave a speech to persuade, even an informal talk to a group. What strategies did you use to adapt to your audience? Were you successful? If not, how could you have increased your success through improved audience analysis?
4. Consider Mandela's credibility as a speaker. What characteristics about him increase the audience's perception of his credibility? How does Mandela use these characteristics in his speech?
5. Think back to a moment when you were in the audience for a persuasive speech. Did you consider the speaker to be credible? Why? If not, what could the speaker have done to increase your perceptions of his or her credibility?
6. Identify the types of power Mandela uses to influence the National Sports Council. How are power and credibility necessarily interwoven? Is it possible to separate them?

**Film:** *The Invitation*
**Year:** 2015
**Central Concept:** Expectancy Violations
**Related Concepts:** Nonverbal Communication, Privacy, Disclosure
**Length and Location of Scene:** Approximately 6 minutes (00:26:00 into 100-minute film)
**Opening Line:** "Seriously, what goes on down there?"
**Closing Line:** "Like Eden said, she's just trying to show you that there's nothing to be afraid of."

**Scene Description:** Following an invitation to attend a dinner party hosted by his ex-wife, Eden (Tammy Blanchard), and her new husband, David (Michiel Huisman), Will (Logan Marshall-Green) rather reluctantly finds himself at his former home with his new girlfriend (Emayatzy Corinealdi) and a select number of friends whom he has not seen since the divorce over two years ago. His flashbacks reveal that Will and Eden's marriage disintegrated after the accidental death of their young son. Will's reservations about Eden's new relationship deepen as the evening progresses, his uncertainty about the nature of the hosts' intentions toward their guests intensified by a series of expectancy violations. In this scene, the group is gathered in the living room to view what some assume will be a recruitment video for The Invitation, the grief support group where Eden and David met.

**Discussion Questions**
1. Describe the various nonverbal responses as the group realizes what it is their hosts are having them view. What is it that Eden ostensibly wants to decrease fear of? How do the subject matter and the hosts' efforts violate social expectations for a dinner party? What other subjects might be considered taboo or inappropriate at a gathering like this?
2. Did all the guests perceive this violation negatively? Describe the range of verbal responses from the different members of the audience. If you had also been a guest, how would this event have made you feel and how would you have responded?
3. Would this have seemed less of a violation had the account simply been described to the group rather than recorded and played back to them as a video? How might social norms of privacy and disclosure affect audience responses in such a situation?

**Film**: *The Iron Lady*
**Year**: 2011
**Central Concept**: Public Speaking
**Related Concepts**: Speaker Credibility, Delivery
**Length and Location of Scene**: Approximately 4 minutes (Chapter 7: 0:40:35–0:44:05)
**Opening Line**: "What is it you took away from your visit, which may be of value here in Great Britain?"
**Closing Line**: "They are absolutely non-negotiable."

**Scene Description**: In *The Iron Lady* Meryl Streep is a tour de force as Margaret Thatcher, the embattled first female Prime Minister of Great Britain. Politics aside, Streep gives a remarkable performance as she demonstrates the challenges that Thatcher experienced, especially as a female leader. Much of the film portrays Thatcher in her later years as a forgetful scion of the old guard who frequently has conversations with her deceased husband. However, interspersed throughout the film are scenes of Thatcher's rise to power and authority. And within those scenes are excellent examples of public speaking, speaker credibility, and leadership.

In this scene, Thatcher is only considering running for the opposing party of Great Britain's Parliament—becoming Prime Minister has not yet crossed her mind. After her two political consultants intently watch an interview that Thatcher gave, they are none too shy about critiquing her performance. They offer advice to improve her credibility and make her resemble a leader with "more importance." Thatcher takes the criticism in stride, offering her own opinion on how the audience sees her. Do you agree with her consultants' advice, or should Thatcher ultimately "just be herself"?

**Note: If you allow the film to run past this scene, we are shown Thatcher receiving voice lessons—a friendly reminder that even polished public speakers need practice.**

### Discussion Questions
1. In your opinion, do you agree that Margaret Thatcher needed to "change her voice" and "get rid of those hats"? Why or why not? How might these qualities influence judgments of her competence, character, and charisma?
2. Concerning the credibility of a speaker, how influential is one's voice to persuade an audience? What about one's appearance? Which particular aspect of delivery (voice, gestures, eye contact, or appearance) is most important for capturing the attention of an audience, and ultimately persuading them?
3. Are the challenges of persuasion different for male and female speakers? How does the context or occasion of the speech influence these challenges? What about the topic of the speech?
4. Recall a speech that you gave to an audience, or a speaker that you witnessed, and analyze the credibility of the speaker (you or someone else). What did you (or the speaker) do to enhance your (or their) credibility in the minds of the audience? Were these strategies successful? Why or why not?

**Film:** *The Joy Luck Club*
**Year:** 1993
**Central Concept:** Culture
**Related Concept:** Communication Competence
**Approximate Scene Location:** 43 minutes into the 138-minute film
**Approximate Scene Length:** 4 minutes
**Opening Line:** "The next week I brought Rich to Mom's birthday dinner." (Waverly's voice)
**Closing Line:** "All this needs is a little soy sauce."

**Scene Description:** Waverly, a Chinese American woman (Tamlyn Tomita), brings her Anglo-American boyfriend Rich (Christopher Rich) home for a dinner cooked by her Chinese mother, Lindo (Tsai Chin). Rich unknowingly insults Waverly's family when he fails to follow the rules of Chinese dining. For instance, he shocks everyone at the table by taking a large first serving of the entree. As Waverly explains in her narration, it is customary in Chinese culture to take only a small spoonful of a dish until everyone else has had some. Rich's biggest mistake is when he misunderstands Lindo's description of her prized entree. Lindo says, "This dish no good. Too salty." Rich decodes the message literally, not paying attention to Lindo's nonverbal cues. The family knows that when Lindo insults her cooking, it means she is pleased with it. The implicit rule is to eat some, then compliment it profusely. Instead, Rich floods the prized dish with soy sauce and assures Lindo that it is not beyond repair.

## Discussion Questions
1. What differences between American and Chinese cultures are depicted in this scene? Use terms from the lecture and text in your analysis.
2. What could Rich have done to enhance his intercultural competence?

**Film**: *The King's Speech*
**Year**: 2010
**Central Concept**: Public Speaking
**Related Concepts**: Stage Fright, Delivery, Articulation
**Length and Location of Scene**: Approximately 4 minutes (exact location 0:34:25–0:38:40)
**Opening Line**: "Strictly business. No personal nonsense."
**Closing Line**: "Father."

**Scene Description**: Colin Firth is Prince Albert (or "Bertie" to his family), the second in line to the throne of England and a man with a bit of a speaking problem. Although Bertie dreads the thought of becoming king and giving public speeches, he accepts the position when his older brother, David, abdicates. Bertie's wife, Queen Elizabeth (Helena Bonham Carter), witnesses her husband struggling to keep his confidence and the public's trust, so she enlists the help of speech therapist Lionel Logue (Geoffrey Rush).

This series of scenes shows Lionel training Bertie in the art of public speaking. Although his methods are unusual, Lionel seems to be making progress with the reluctant King. The audience can only hope that Lionel's unorthodox techniques will cure the King of his "bloody stammer" and instill the poise he needs to lead England.

## Discussion Questions
1. What is your opinion of Lionel's strategies to help the King? Do you believe these strategies would really be effective in reducing his stage fright? Why or why not?
2. How common is stage fright for the average person who is about to give a speech? Do you know anyone, either famous or otherwise, who experiences stage fright?
3. What techniques do you use to manage your own stage fright before, and even during, a public speech? How successful have you been with these techniques?
4. Analyze your own delivery skills. Which parts of your delivery give you confidence? Which parts would you like to improve?

**Film**: *Lincoln*
**Year**: 2012
**Central Concept**: Public Speaking
**Related Concepts**: Persuasion, Narrative Style, Ethos/Pathos/Logos, Delivery
**Length and Location of Scene**: Approximately 7 minutes (Chapter 4: 0:23:20–0:30:50)
**Opening Line**: "Thunder forth, God of War."
**Closing Line**: "And come February the first, I intend to sign the Thirteenth Amendment!"

**Scene Description**: In this stirring and critically acclaimed film about Abraham Lincoln (Daniel Day-Lewis), Director Steven Spielberg recounts the president's challenges leading up to passage of the Thirteenth Amendment to abolish slavery. The film takes an intimate look at Lincoln, peeling back the tableau of his fabled presidency to reveal a man deeply devoted to his family, to his country, and to his morals. Passing the Thirteenth Amendment to the Constitution was no easy task. Indeed, history tells us that Lincoln had to use every persuasive tactic at his disposal to convince—some might say bribe, cajole, and harass—his fellow politicians to support the bill. While history recognizes President Lincoln as a great public orator, the film also illustrates his formidable rhetorical skills in smaller groups, interpersonally and one on one. Imagine if the freedom of an entire race were resting on your shoulders. Would you have the communication skills to persuade your audience?

Although it is not one of Abraham Lincoln's traditional public speeches (i.e., one person speaking to many people), this scene illustrates the various tactics he used to persuade others. Pay close attention to the structure of Lincoln's talk, and the reactions of his audience. Likewise, notice how he effectively weaves together ethical, emotional, and logical forms of proof. Not only is this scene an example of persuasive rhetoric, it is also a helpful lesson in American history.

**Discussion Questions**
1. What effect does Lincoln's use of narrative (i.e., the opening story) have on his audience? Is his speech more or less persuasive because of the narrative structure?
2. Recall an occasion when you listened to a speaker tell a story as part of the speech. What effect did the story have on you? Can narratives and stories be used ineffectively in public speaking? How so?
3. Does President Lincoln use humor effectively in his speech? Why or why not?
4. Have you ever attempted to use humor in one of your speeches? How effective was it in gaining the attention of your audience? What about persuading your audience?
5. Use Aristotle's three forms of proof (ethos, pathos, and logos) to analyze Lincoln's speech. Which form of proof seems to stand out the most? Was it effective? Why?
6. What aspects of Lincoln's delivery influence the outcome of his speech? Please explain.

**Film**: *McFarland, USA* (2 scenes)
**Year**: 2015
**Central Concept**: Intercultural Competence
**Related Concepts**: Stereotypes, Prejudice, Collectivistic Culture, Culture Shock

**Length and Location of Scene 1**: Approximately 2 minutes (00:07:10 into 129-minute film)
**Opening Line**: "Hi." "Hello. How are you?" "Good." "Good."
**Closing Line**: "You know what. We're not staying."
**Length and Location of Scene 2**: Approximately 4 minutes (00:64:05 into film)
**Opening Line**: Chickens clucking in front yard.
**Closing Line**: "You know you're white, right?"

**Scene #1 Description:** Following a series of incidents that cost him a number of jobs, football coach Jim White (Kevin Costner) is relegated to accepting a position at a high school in McFarland, USA, one of the poorest cities in the country. In this predominantly Latino community, the aptly named White (or Blanco as the locals initially call him) will eventually build a rewarding new life for himself, for his family, and for many of the students he coaches. This is a heartwarming Disney sports movie based on an inspiring true story. When the White family steps out for dinner on their first night in town, however, McFarland does not appear to hold great promise for a happily ever after.

**Discussion Questions**
1. What aspects of their new community contribute to the Whites' sense of culture shock? What might they have done to mitigate this initial experience? How could they have improved their intercultural competence in advance of their move?
2. Although the interaction when they order their food is friendly, the atmosphere becomes tense when they leave the restaurant. Why does the mood change? What stereotypes or prejudices might account in part for this tension?

**Scene 2 Description:** Moving on from football, Coach White creates and nurtures a cross-country team of seven Latino students whose physical and mental stamina, derived from a life of laboring as farm pickers, he hopes to translate into athletic success. After discovering, however, that three of his runners, the Diaz brothers, may have quit the team, he decides to pay a visit to the family at home, where he is invited in for dinner.

**Discussion Questions**
1. Although White has by this point become a more integrated and valued member of the McFarland community, he still has a lot to learn about Latino culture. Interacting with the Diaz family at their home helps correct which of White's enduring cultural misconceptions and stereotypes?
2. Describe the many ways this scene illustrates a collectivistic culture.
3. Discuss the importance of increased contact with other cultures on the road to overcoming prejudice and increasing intercultural competence. Does this scene support the adage that the best way to know a culture is through their food? In what other ways can we increase our intercultural knowledge? What action does White take at the end of this scene to increase his exposure and understanding, and what do you think he will learn as a result of this experience?

26

**Film:** *Nightcrawler*
**Year:** 2014
**Central Concept:** Media Ethics
**Related Concepts:** Agenda Setting, Privacy
**Length and Location of Scene:** Approximately 4 minutes (00:17:15 minutes into 117-minute film)
**Opening Line:** "Excuse me. I have video footage."
**Closing Line:** "I believe you."

**Scene Description:** This scene depicts Lou Bloom's first successful foray into L.A. crime reporting. A petty thief in search of more secure, though not necessarily more ethical, employment, Bloom (Jake Gyllenhaal) happens upon a freelance journalist filming the police pulling a woman from a car wreck, nightcrawler footage for local news stations. Unperturbed by the horror of the scene but excited by its income potential, Bloom is inspired to pursue a new career, which he does by stealing a high-end bike to finance his purchase of a camcorder and police radio scanner. Bloom is highly driven and wholly unscrupulous, a combination that is well suited to advancing in his chosen profession. When he takes graphic footage of a fatal carjacking to the local TV station, he meets Nina Romina (Rene Russo), a KWLA 6 news producer who, recognizing his raw talent and ambition, takes him under her journalistic wing.
**Note: This scene features a graphic video of the dying victim.**

**Discussion Questions**
1. Explain how this scene confirms the old news adage "if it bleeds, it leads." The theory of agenda setting argues that media coverage of an issue determines its salience for the public. How does the media's coverage of crime affect our perception of it?
2. Assistant editor Frank Kruse disagrees with Nina's decision to air Bloom's piece, deeming the footage "excessive." How would you describe Bloom's video, and do you agree with Frank or with Nina about its broadcast worthiness?
3. Are there any circumstances that justify filming a victim's death or dead body for later public viewing? When does the public's right to know override the individual's right to privacy?
4. Nina explains to Lou that their viewers favor footage of victims who are "preferably well-off and white, injured at the hands of the poor or a minority." From what you have observed about news content, do you agree with her assessment of KWLA 6's audience? If so, what does this say about the ethics of her audience and the station?

**Film**: *The Perks of Being a Wallflower*
**Year**: 2012
**Central Concept**: Communication Competence
**Related Concepts**: Emotional Expression, Honesty, Self-Disclosure, Relational Dialectics
**Length and Location of Scene**: Approximately 4 minutes (Chapter 14: 1:03:10–1:07:13)
**Opening Line**: "Things are a total disaster."
**Closing Line**: "What the hell is wrong with you?"

**Scene Description**: In this coming-of-age film based on a book of the same name, Charlie (Logan Lerman) has always struggled to fit in. Painfully shy and introverted since he was a little boy, Charlie is now a freshman in high school—an easy target for bullies. Fortunately for him, two seniors (Patrick [Ezra Miller] and Sam [Emma Watson]) take Charlie under their wing and educate him on the finer principles of high school social life. As Charlie expands his horizons—forming lasting friendships, going to parties, and even experiencing his first kiss—his identity slowly becomes more transparent and engaging. Still, Charlie is troubled by his past. He keeps a dark secret buried deep in his psyche, a secret so unfathomable that his mind has hidden it from himself. When Charlie is finally able to comprehend what happened to him, he needs complete support from his family and his first real friends: Patrick and Sam.

In this two-part scene Charlie has started dating Mary Elizabeth (Mae Whitman), a mutual friend of Patrick and Sam. To say that Charlie feels suffocated and controlled by Mary Elizabeth would be an understatement. In the first half of this scene, witness as Charlie pretends to be happy in their relationship. As Charlie is new to the rules of dating, he does not know how to end the relationship—he doesn't even realize that breaking up is an option. In the second part of the scene, Charlie's inexperience and lack of emotional intelligence become quite obvious. Will his friends forgive him for his brutally honest self-disclosure?

**Discussion Questions**
1. **Watch the scene up until 1:05:15 and pause it.** How would you describe the relationship between Charlie and Mary Elizabeth? Which relational dialectics are causing tension for Charlie? How is he managing this tension?
2. Is their relationship symmetrical or complementary? Have you ever seen, or perhaps experienced, a relationship like theirs? Did both parties experience relational satisfaction? Please explain.
3. You might argue that Charlie is committing the fallacy of approval: the irrational behavior of seeking everyone else's approval, even to the point of sacrificing one's own happiness. Speculate and analyze why someone might experience this fallacy.
4. **Continue watching the remainder of the scene.** How would you describe Charlie's emotional intelligence? Was his expression of honesty justified? Please explain.
5. If you were Charlie's friend, what advice would you give him about appropriate self-disclosure, emotional expression, and dating?

**Film**: *Pitch Perfect*
**Year**: 2012
**Central Concept**: Perception
**Related Concepts**: Perception Process, Stereotyping, Culture, Identity
**Length and Location of Scene**: Approximately 5 minutes (Chapter 2: 0:08:50–0:14:15)
**Opening Line**: "That's a double-negative."
**Closing Line**: "What are we going to do?"

**Scene Description**: *Pitch Perfect* is *Mean Girls* meets *Glee*, with a dash of *Best in Show* sprinkled on top—only with human performers, not dogs. Becca (Anna Kendrick) is the new kid on campus, searching for an identity and a reason to be in college. It doesn't help that her overly protective father is a professor at the same school, or that her new roommate is more than slightly intimidating. Indeed, Becca would rather be anywhere but here. With her talent for mixing musical genres, she aspires to be a music producer, not a college freshman. Much to own her surprise, Becca auditions for an all-female a cappella group on campus: the Barden Bellas. The Bellas, after a disastrous performance last year, have their own reputation to salvage. Can Becca's mastery of musical mashups catapult the Bellas to singing success, or is this misfit collection of performers destined to fall flat?

This scene finds Becca, and other characters, wandering around the college's Activities Faire. As the name suggests, the Activities Faire is a showcase of different clubs, groups, and organizations on campus. And as one might expect, each group has its own unique . . . well, let's just say that each group is different. Observe the characteristics of these groups, how they are seen and how they see themselves, and how this influences their communication.

**Discussion Questions**
1. How does the perception process (selection, organization, and interpretation) influence the characters' communication with each other?
2. In what ways do the characters engage in stereotyping? What is the basis for these group stereotypes?
3. How does each group demonstrate its own unique culture?
4. Think about the school clubs you belong to now, those you belonged to in high school, or those clubs you knew about. What were the perceptions of these clubs? Why? How did those perceptions influence the ways members were treated by people outside the club?
5. How did being part of a group—an official club or even a social group—influence your identity? Did you find yourself taking on the qualities of the group? How so?

**Film:** *Precious*
**Year:** 2009
**Central Concept:** Self-Disclosure
**Related Concepts:** Emotional Expression, Ego-boosting, Listening
**Approximate Scene Location:** 83 minutes into the 109-minute movie
**Approximate Scene Length:** 3 minutes
**Opening Line:** "Come with me."
**Closing Line:** "Write."

**Scene Description:** Precious (Gabourey Sidibe) is a 16-year-old who has suffered abuse at the hands of both of her parents. By this scene, Precious has given birth to a second child by her father, who has repeatedly raped her. After her mother turns her abuse to the baby, Precious finally leaves. Precious has been attending an alternative school where her class has become her family, and she is finally learning to read and write. In this scene, Precious is unable to write in her journal, a regular and welcome assignment; pushed to disclose what is bothering her, she receives affirmation from her teacher.

## Discussion Questions
1. What prompts Precious to self-disclose? What was the effect of her self-disclosure?
2. Precious gives examples of what she thinks are supposed to be "love"; how might she have gotten to the point where she thinks of these as examples of love?
3. What effect do you think Ms. Rain's affirmation toward Precious might have on her self-esteem? How might it affect her future relationship with her son?

**Film:** *Selma*
**Year:** 2014
**Central Concept:** Relational Messages
**Related Concept:** Language
**Approximate Scene Location:** 9 minutes into the 128-minute movie
**Approximate Scene Length:** 4.5 minutes
**Opening Line:** "Mr. President, Dr. King."
**Closing Line:** "Yes, Mr. President, I understand."

**Scene Description:** In this scene, Dr. Martin Luther King Jr. (played by David Oyelowo) is meeting with President Johnson (played by Tom Wilkinson), discussing the civil rights movement. The President verbally expresses a desire to help, and Dr. King has a very clear description as to what should happen next. While appearing to be amenable to further progress, President Johnson tries to change the subject and to put off the topic of voting. While Dr. King is respectful of the Office of the President, he is direct in his observations, and doesn't allow the subject of voting rights to be dropped.

## Discussion Questions
1. What relational messages are being sent by the nonverbal in this scene? What can we interpret about how these two men feel about each other?
2. The President and Dr. King have different goals in this scene. How do they each use their language to achieve their goals? Which way do you think was more effective?
3. Discuss a situation in which you had a goal to accomplish, but you were communicating with someone who had a competing goal that he was trying to accomplish. How did you try to achieve your goal? How did you react when the other person was trying to achieve his goal?

**Film**: *The Social Network*
**Year**: 2010
**Central Concept**: Social Media and Communication Competence
**Related Concepts**: Communication Channels, Emotions, Relational Quality, Conflict
**Length and Location of Scene**: 1 minute, 08 seconds (YouTube Channel; exact location 0:52:20–0:53:28)
**Opening Line:** "Could I talk to you alone for a second?"
**Closing Line:** "Good luck with your video game."

**Scene Description**: Facebook creator Mark Zuckerberg (Jesse Eisenberg) demonstrates that while he may be a genius at computer programming and meeting the needs of the marketplace, he is a disaster in the domain of personal relationships. In this scene, Erica Albright (Rooney Mara) confronts Mark about how poorly he treated her and the dangers of using the Internet to communicate his views.

**Discussion Questions**

1. When Erica told Mark that the Internet wasn't written in pencil but in ink, how well do you think he understood the permanent nature of the medium that, ironically, had brought him so much success?
2. Do you agree with Erica that we choose technology to express our negative emotions over other channels more often today?
3. Describe the balance between using face-to-face and social media to communicate in your relationships with others. After assessing the advantages and drawbacks, could that balance be shifted to improve how completely you communicate with someone? How?
4. Analyze an example of using social media from your own life that wasn't communicated competently. What role did the medium play? How could you have communicated your message competently?

**Film**: *Thank You for Smoking*
**Year**: 2006
**Central Concept**: Persuasion
**Related Concepts**: Ethos/Pathos/Logos, Social Judgment Theory, Fallacies of Reasoning, Ethics
**Approximate Scene Location**: 45 minutes into the 92-minute film
**Approximate Scene Length**: 5 minutes
**Opening Line**: "Pearl, we got company."
**Closing Line**: "No, Lorne. Either you keep all the money, or you give it all away."

**Scene Description**: Based on the novel by Christopher Buckley, this film is a satirical look at both the tobacco industry and the congressional lobbying system. Nick Naylor (Aaron Eckhart) is the Vice President and lead spokesperson for the Academy of Tobacco Studies, an oxymoronic institution if there ever was one. Nick's job—at which he is quite successful—is to persuade whoever is listening that smoking cigarettes is not unhealthy. The film illustrates a variety of fallacious and morally questionable persuasive strategies. In this scene, Nick has been dispatched by big tobacco to the home of the actor who portrayed the Marlboro Man in cigarette ads. Now the actor is dying of lung cancer, and Nick is there to bribe him to keep quiet. What ensues is a clever example of illogical reasoning and unethical persuasion.

**Discussion Questions**

1. Provide examples of ethos, pathos, and logos appeals Nick made in his conversation with the Marlboro Man.
2. Use social judgment theory to explain how Nick successfully persuades the Marlboro Man to take the bribe. Given his high ego-involvement, plot out the Marlboro Man's latitudes of acceptance, rejection, and noncommitment, and arrange Nick's arguments along that continuum.

3. Describe three fallacies of reasoning that Nick uses in his argument. Why did the Marlboro Man not see these fallacies? Which fallacies have you found to be used most often in real-world examples, based on your personal observations?
4. In Nick's own words, his job requires "a moral flexibility" that most people don't have; in other words, it's unethical. Discuss additional, real-world examples of persuasion that you have found to be unethical.

**Film**: *Trust*
**Year**: 2010
**Central Concept**: Self-Disclosure
**Related Concepts**: Privacy Management, Family Communication, Communication Climate
**Length and Location of Scene**: Approximately 3 minutes (Chapter 9: 1:15:30–1:18:44)
**Opening Line**: "Kids! Hurry up, the food's going to be cold."
**Closing Line**: "Let me go!"

**Scene Description**: *Trust* is the sobering account of one family's struggle to remain intact following the rape of their daughter, Annie (Liana Liberato). The film begins with a series of fairly innocuous and seemingly harmless scenes of text messages between 14-year-old Annie and her cyber-friend, Charlie. Initially Annie and Charlie meet in a chat room about sports. Over the course of several months, and hundreds of texts, they become very close to one another—in fact, Annie develops a crush on Charlie entirely through text messages. Charlie first claims that he is 16 years old; later on he changes his story to 20, and finally he says he is 25 years old. Despite having been lied to, Annie agrees to meet Charlie in a public place, where she discovers that his age is actually closer to 35. In a disturbing scene Charlie seduces and rapes Annie in his hotel room. The rest of the film wrestles with the aftermath of this crime, including the effects on Annie, her friends, and her family.

In a scene prior to this one, Annie explicitly demanded that her father (Will, played by Clive Owen) not tell her brother (Peter, played by Spencer Curnutt) about what happened to her; Peter has been away at college during the incident. Here, Annie and her family are gathered around the dinner table, discussing their plans and costumes for Halloween. Almost immediately Annie notices that her family is speaking to her in an unexpected manner, and she soon realizes that everyone else knows about what happened to her. Annie confronts her father about violating her privacy, setting off a chain reaction of broken trust, hurt feelings, and conflict.
**Note: Additional scenes from this film can also be used to illustrate privacy and self-disclosure as well, especially scenes with Annie, her therapist, and her parents.**

**Discussion Questions**
1. Describe the communication climate of this scene, from the beginning to the end, and identify examples of confirming and disconfirming messages directed toward Annie. How does Annie perceive these messages? Confirming? Disconfirming? Why?

2. As the owner of this private information, does Annie have a right to keep her disclosures private from other family members? Why or why not? Did her father violate Annie's privacy, or can his revealing of her disclosure be justified?

3. Recall a moment in your life when you felt that your private disclosure was violated. Was your disclosure revealed intentionally or accidentally? Did you establish any rules with the recipient prior to your disclosure? What did you learn from the experience?

4. What is this particular scene mostly about: self-disclosure, privacy, or communication climate? Please explain and justify your answer with examples.

**Film:** *The Wolf of Wall Street*
**Year:** 2013
**Central Concept:** Persuasion, Organizational Communication
**Related Concepts:** Public Speaking, Ethos/Pathos/Logos
**Length and Location of Scene:** Approximately 6 minutes (1:19:00 into 180-minute film)
**Opening Line:** "For those of you who don't know me, my name's Steve Madden."
**Closing Line:** "Now let's knock this *#$@! out of the park."

**Scene Description:** Based on a memoir, Martin Scorsese's biopic charts the rise and fall of Jordan Belfort (Leonardo DiCaprio), who succumbs to various kinds of temptation, excess, and corruption while climbing the Wall Street ladder of success. In this scene, Belfort, still at the top of his game of greed, delivers a motivational speech peppered with profanity to employees at Stratton Oakmont, a brokerage firm he founded upon the professed values of "stability, integrity, pride." The company's ethical façade was expressly created to attract the gullible in need of a guide through the investment jungle, his characterization of the stock market for prospective clients.

Speaking to staff, however, he abandons all pretense. On the launch of the biggest IPO in the organization's history, his purpose is simple—rouse the troops to lucrative acts of telephone terrorism, namely, per Belfort's directive, ramming Steve Madden (Jake Hoffman) stock down clients' throats. To that end, the firm's CEO demonstrates the qualities that enabled him to excel in sales and proves that inspiration can take many oratorical forms. Belfort successfully appeals on a number of rhetorical fronts to an audience in whom he has apparently cultivated similar values. Madden, a relatively unknown designer at this point, speaks to far less stirring effect. **Note: The scene contains language that may offend some viewers.**

**Discussion Questions**
1. How does the audience respond to Madden's self-introduction? How does Belfort coach Madden from the sidelines? How does Belfort attempt to enhance Madden's image and credibility when he subsequently takes the floor to speak?

2. Evaluate the persuasive appeals of each speaker in terms of ethos, pathos, and logos. Consider both verbal and nonverbal dimensions of their communication. How does the apparent corporate culture at Stratton Oakmont contribute to Belfort's success as an orator?

3. Research indicates that swearing can increase solidarity and promote a sense of connection among bosses and coworkers. Have you ever heard raunchy rhetoric at the workplace? From whom, a boss or a coworker? How did this make you feel?

# SECTION II
# TELEVISION PROGRAMS

Each of the television program entries in this section provides information in the following categories:

*TV Show Data:* Year, Number of Seasons, Creator(s), Genre, and Episode Length
*Characters/Actors:* Principal actors and roles in the program
*Communication Concepts*: Primary communication topics in the program (listed alphabetically)
*TV Show Storyline*: General background and potential warning information about the television program, as well as a brief summary of its plot and themes.
*Discussion Questions*: Questions (and answers to the first two) linking the film to communication concepts

The following are a number of television programs that have human communication as a central theme. The discussion questions that follow the basic data about the program are the heart of this section. The questions posed are not the only ones that can or should be asked, nor is there only one "right" way to respond to the questions. In fact, you may argue with some of the analyses and interpretations. That's fine—any good discussion about television programs should engender disagreement. The questions are provided simply to offer an example of how to analyze the program and the communication that goes on within it.

# THE BIG BANG THEORY

| TV Show Data | |
|---|---|
| Year Began | 2007 |
| Number of Seasons | 9 |
| Creator(s) | Chuck Lorre, Bill Prady |
| Genre | Situation Comedy |
| Episode Length | 30 minutes |

| Main Cast | |
|---|---|
| **Character** | **Actor** |
| Leonard Hofstadter | Johnny Galecki |
| Sheldon Cooper | Jim Parsons |
| Penny | Kaley Cuoco |
| Howard Wolowitz | Simon Helberg |
| Raj Koothrappali | Kunal Nayyar |
| Bernadette Rostenkowski | Melissa Rauch |
| Amy Farrah Fowler | Mayim Bialik |
| Stuart Bloom | Kevin Sussman |

## TV Show Storyline

Described as a TV show "like *Friends* but for nerds," *The Big Bang Theory* is a 30-minute sitcom that began in 2007. The show revolves around the lives of four extremely intelligent, and socially awkward, scientists who work at Caltech University. Leonard and Sheldon, both physicists, are roommates, while Raj (an astrophysicist) and Howard (an aerospace engineer) are their friends and colleagues. The theme of the show explores the general geekiness of the characters, including their poor interpersonal skills, their disturbingly strong penchant for quoting Star Trek, and their shared belief that science can solve any problem. Across the hall from Leonard and Sheldon lives Penny, an aspiring actress who currently waitresses to make ends meet. With her street smarts and advanced social skills, Penny is the perfect foil for the four men. In fact, Penny intrigues Leonard so much that they start dating and develop a romantic relationship. The other two recurring characters, Bernadette and Amy, also work at Caltech, and they become romantically involved with Howard and Sheldon, respectively.

**Note: The location of each scene is based on viewing the episode without commercials (e.g., Amazon Instant Video, Hulu Plus, iTunes). Each episode is approximately 22 minutes in length.**

## *Season 6, Episode 6: "The Extract Obliteration"*

Unrelated to the title of this episode, the scene for analysis involves Leonard and Sheldon. Recently, Penny revealed to Leonard that she enrolled in a history course at the local community college. And despite her concern that Leonard would "make a big deal" about it, she tells him that she wrote a paper for the class. When Leonard secretly reads Penny's paper—even though he promised he wouldn't—he needs advice about what to do next. Obviously desperate, Leonard asks Sheldon for help. However, Sheldon has his own interpersonal dilemma: his new online friend, astrophysicist Stephen Hawking, has not been in contact for days. Needless to say, Sheldon has some difficulty being an active listener for Leonard.

**Central Concept**: Listening
**Related Concept**: Perception Checking
**Length and Location of Scene**: Exactly 3 minutes (0:10:50–0:13:50)
**Opening Line**: "Play. Play. Play."
**Closing Line**: "Oh, of course, it only works on the weak-minded."

**Discussion Questions**
1. Identify and describe Leonard's listening style compared to Sheldon's. Are both of their listening responses competent? Why or why not?
2. What do you think about Leonard's solution to use a chess clock? Would the clock encourage active or pseudo listening? Please explain.
3. Leonard outlines two rules of their conversation: they take turns, and each turn includes a response from the friend. How similar are Leonard's rules to the process of perception checking? Compare and contrast the scene with what you have learned about perception checking.
4. When have you encountered poor listeners in your own experiences? Are there certain situations or contexts that discourage active listening? Are certain people simply better listeners than others?

## *Season 6, Episode 17: "The Monster Isolation"*

The scene for analysis in this episode once again illustrates Sheldon's incompetent communication. We see Sheldon recording an online video in what appears to be a long-running series about flags—yes, flags, their history, their colors, even alternate uses for them. Sheldon discusses all of these topics on "Fun with Flags." To help illustrate how to spark a conversation about flags, Sheldon employs Penny's assistance. However, Penny notices that Sheldon's nonverbal cues are a bit rigid and she gives him some tips about "how to be more open in front of the camera." Naturally, Sheldon takes her advice a bit too far.

**Central Concept**: Nonverbal Communication
**Length and Location of Scene**: Approximately 3 minutes (0:02:20–0:05:35)
**Opening Line**: "Hello. I am Dr. Sheldon Cooper."
**Closing Line**: "Spread your legs; invite them in."

**Discussion Questions**
1.  Identify the different types of nonverbal communication shown in this scene.
2.  Which functions of nonverbal communication does Sheldon demonstrate? What meanings would most people attach to Sheldon's nonverbal cues?
3.  Like Sheldon, even competent communicators sometimes misinterpret nonverbal cues. Think of a moment in your life when you had difficulty with nonverbal communication, either as the sender or the receiver. What happened? Why did miscommunication occur?

## *Season 6, Episode 18: "The Contractual Obligation Implementation"*

In this episode, Raj is experiencing some serious dating problems. His most recent date, Lucy, snuck away by climbing out of a bathroom window! It seems that Lucy suffers from social anxiety disorder, and going out on dates is a bit of a challenge for her. Undaunted, Raj continues to pursue Lucy and she finally agrees to another date. This time Raj has a plan to make the date less stressful for Lucy: it is a texting date and she will not have to talk to Raj in order to communicate. Ironically, Raj's creative solution might be an unfortunate reality for many daters today.

**Central Concept**: Technology
**Related Concepts**: Computer-Mediated Communication
**Length and Location of Scene 1**: Approximately 1 minute (0:09:40–0:10:55)
**Opening Line**: "Excuse me, I'm meeting a girl here."
**Closing Line**: "I have an adorable accent."

**Discussion Questions**
1.  Although creative, Raj's solution to managing Lucy's dating anxiety is not entirely unprecedented. Describe how you use technology (e.g., texting) before, during, and after a date. Is texting the preferred mode of communication to arrange a date?
2.  If you have ever been in a long-distance relationship, or know someone who has, then it's likely that you have seen the pros and cons of using technology to maintain the relationship. In a long-distance relationship, what are the pros of using text messages to communicate with your partner? What are the cons?

**Length and Location of Scene 2**: Approximately 2 minutes (0:14:25–0:16:05)
**Opening Line**: "My dad's a gynecologist in India."
**Closing Line**: "That was supposed to say that I like sports."

**Discussion Questions**
1. How frequently do misunderstandings occur via text messages? What have you learned that can help you avoid these misunderstandings?
2. Does texting have some benefits compared with face-to-face conversations? Make a list of these benefits and compare your list with someone else's.
3. What is in store for the future of technology and dating? Speculate what dating might be like 5 or 10 years from now. Will there be a greater reliance on technology? Possibly less?

# BLACK MIRROR

| TV Show Data | |
|---|---|
| Year Began | 2011 |
| Number of Seasons | 4 |
| Creator | Charlie Brooker |
| Genre | Science fiction, horror |
| Episode Length | ~ 60 minutes |

| Main Cast (S03 E01: "Nosedive") | |
|---|---|
| **Character** | **Actor** |
| Lacie Pound | Bryce Dallas Howard |
| Alice Eve | Naomi Jayne Blestow |
| Cherry Jones | Susan |
| James Norton | Ryan Pound |
| Alan Ritchson | Paul |
| Daisy Haggard | Bets |
| Susannah Fielding | Carol |
| Demetri Goritsas | Hansen |
| Kadiff Kirwin | Chester |
| Soper Dirisu | Man in jail |

| Main Cast (S03 E04: "San Junipero") | |
|---|---|
| **Character** | **Actor** |
| Kelly Booth | Gugu Mbatha-Raw |
| Yorkie | Mackenzie Davis |
| Elder Kelly | Denise Burse |
| Greg | Raymond McAnally |
| Wes | Gavin Stenhouse |
| Laura | Cheryl Anderson |
| Harvey | Jackson Bews |
| Elder Yorkie | Annabel Davis |

"This place ain't for the faint hearted"—a tweet from Black Mirror promoting the episode "Black Museum"—captures the mood of most episodes, which even seasoned critics have acknowledged can sometimes be too bleak to bear. Yet grim is not merely gratuitous in stories intended to instruct as they entertain, the conclusion for the series teaser signalss both its tone and its objective: "Welcome to the darkness. We hope you find it enlightening." The titular black mirror refers to the shiny monitors on our digital devices—TV, tablet, and smartphone screens that significantly, when dark, reflect the user's image. *The Twilight Zone* for the 21st century, *Black Mirror* offers various cautionary tales of a techno-dystopia, imagined presents or near-futures in which new communication technologies (NCTs), as directed by the worst of human impulses, create new perils for unsuspecting cybercitizens.
**Note: This series contains strong language.**

## *Season 3, Episode 1: "Nosedive"*

"Nosedive" follows the exploits of Lacie Pound in her intensified campaign to raise her rating on a social media app that rates people from 4.2, where we find her initially, to the higher 4-point echelon on a 5-point scale. External validation conveyed in the quantification of others defines the self in an America where everybody grades everybody else on every (typically insignificant) thing, and augmented-reality contact lenses make your holistic rating as a person visible whenever someone looks at you. Popularity so measured provides not just social capital but a plethora of privilege. A high-4 rating confers status and advantage in the form of better cars, flights, jobs, homes, and healthcare. Lacie, discontentedly living with her 3.0 brother (Ryan), is desperately chasing a 4.5 rating to qualify for a 20 percent discount on rent in a more upscale community. When she reconnects on this app with a childhood frenemy (Naomi Jayne Blestow), a 4.8 social media star who unexpectedly asks Lacie to be maid of honor at her posh wedding, those 0.3 points are suddenly within her grasp. But, as the title suggests, upward is not the social trajectory dramatized in this episode.

**Central Concepts**: Computer-Mediated Communication/Technology/Social Media
**Related Concepts**: Uses and Gratifications Theory, Emotions, Persuasive Appeals
**Length and Location of Scene 1**: Approximately 2 minutes (~ 0:06:20–0:8:27)
**Opening Line**: Lacie interrupts work at her place of employment, shifting silently from her business computer screen to her social media app once her smartphone alert rings.
**Closing Line**: "Of course, if it drops below 2.5, then it's bye-bye."
**Length and Location of Scene 2**: Approximately 4 minutes (~ 0:21:55–0:25:57)
**Opening Line**: "In this world, we're all so caught up in our own heads."
**Closing Line**: "That's great. Just great."

**Discussion Questions**
1. Applying uses and gratifications theory, describe the role of social media for Lacey.
2. Provide specific examples of how Lacey's addiction to social media affects virtually every aspect of her life.

3. Describe Lacey's emotions suggested by her nonverbal communication as she checks her number on this social app and then looks at Naomi's postings and ratings. Research has linked Facebook use to depression. Why might this be the case for some users?
4. At one point, Ryan opines to Lacie, "I am sorry, but I miss the normal you. Before this obsession when we had conversations, remember?" How does computer-mediated communication differ from face-to-face interaction? Consider the advantages and disadvantages of each.
5. Which of the three persuasive appeals (ethos, pathos, or logos) figures excessively in Lacey's wedding speech? Have you heard another speech that overdid it in a similar manner?

## *Season 3, Episode 4: "San Junipero"*

Emmy Award winner for Outstanding Television Movie, this episode is also distinguished by an uncharacteristically happy ending for *Black Mirror*, although what exactly that ending entails remains a matter of Internet debate. In the first scene, a naïve twenty-something (Yorkie) meets a street-smart 1980s party girl (Kelly) at a dance club in San Junipero, where (major spoiler alert) they begin a time-traveling love affair that we later discover is a product of virtual reality. Jumping ahead to the story's enigmatic conclusion, Kelly and Yorkie argue about the best way to end one's life, or continue it indefinitely, as the case may be. Sci-fi technology in this episode can upload your consciousness to the cloud, offering the option of life-after-death in San Junipero or another virtual reality of your choice. But will Kelly decide to pursue this alternative and continue her virtual relationship with Yorkie?

**Central Concepts**: Computer-Mediated Communication/Technology
**Related Concepts**: Virtual Reality, Persuasive Appeals, Perception, Identity Management
**Length and Location of Scene 1**: Approximately 1 minute (~ 0:05:55–0:6:56)
**Opening Line**: "What are you doing?"
**Closing Line**: "Thanks. Cheers."
**Length and Location of Scene 2**: Approximately 5 minutes (~ 0:49:00–0:54:00)
**Opening Line**: "Hey, you didn't dress up to see me?"
**Closing Line**: "Kelly, I'm sorry."

**Discussion Questions**
1. What role do *fashion statements*, a term Kelly invokes at the dance club, play in perception and identity management?
2. Describe the different persuasive appeals to ethos, pathos, and logos that Kelly and Yorkie use in their later arguments for and against San Junipero.
3. Whose position do you support and why? In an imagined future that made San Junipero an option, would you choose virtual reality as your final destination?
4. As the credits roll at the end of this episode, viewers see Yorkie and Kelly drive off together into a San Junipero sunset, a scene widely interpreted to mean that Kelly changes her mind after the scene where they argue. Other Internet fans disagree, positing this is a less authentic computer-generated version of the real Kelly, who, like her husband, ultimately rejected a digital afterlife. Do you support this theory? Would communication with any virtual surrogate of a loved one be better than no communication at all?

# BREAKING BAD

| TV Show Data | |
|---|---|
| Year Began | 2008 |
| Number of Seasons | 5 |
| Creator(s) | Vince Gilligan |
| Genre | Crime Drama |
| Episode Length | 47 Minutes |

| Main Cast | |
|---|---|
| **Character** | **Actor** |
| Walter White | Bryan Cranston |
| Skylar White | Anna Gunn |
| Jesse Pinkman | Aaron Paul |
| Hank Schrader | Dean Norris |
| Marie Schrader | Betsy Brandt |
| Walter White Jr. | RJ Mitte |

## TV Show Storyline

*Breaking Bad* is known for its powerful writing and fervent following. The show begins with Walter White, a brilliant high school chemistry teacher barely able to support his newly pregnant wife and teenage son. Shortly after turning 50, he is diagnosed with inoperable lung cancer. With nothing left to lose, he decides to start using his chemistry knowledge to cook meth and provide financially for his family. While on a ride-along with his DEA brother-in-law, Walt sees a former student, Jesse Pinkman, run from a crime scene and recognizes him. Walt then blackmails him into going into business with him.

**Note: This series contains strong language.**

**Note: The location of each scene is based on viewing the episode without commercials (e.g., Amazon Instant Video, Hulu Plus, iTunes, Netflix). Each episode is approximately 47 minutes in length.**

## Season 1, Episode 1: "Pilot"

In this first scene for analysis, Walt and Jesse are just starting their meth-cooking partnership. Walt steals some equipment from the high school, and Jesse seems unimpressed with Walt's technical approach. This scene highlights the very different characters, and their different approaches to the same concepts—while cooking meth.

**Central Concepts**: Self-Concept, Language
**Related Concepts**: Perception, Identity Management
**Length and Location of Scene 1**: Approximately 2 minutes (0:32:10–0:34:14)
**Opening Line**: "You just going to sit there?"
**Closing Line**: ". . . not me!"

### Discussion Questions
1. How does Jesse react to being told what to do by Walt?
2. Does their conversation change their teacher/student dynamic?
3. How are they using language to convey their identities?

## Season 3, Episode 10: "Fly"

In this scene, Walt and Jesse are in the middle of a "cook" when Walt finds a fly in the lab. Walt is trying to convince Jesse that the fly is a problem. This scene highlights Walt's and Jesse's use of language, as well as how nonverbals communicate relational messages.

**Central Concepts**: Power, Relational Messages
**Related Concepts**: Language, Nonverbal Messages
**Length and Location of Scene 2**: Approximately 5 minutes (0:11:10–0:16:25)
**Opening Line**: "There's been a contamination."
**Closing Line**: "Okay."

### Discussion Questions
1. Walt and Jess seem to have some confusion about the problem. How do they express their confusion? What do you think was the cause of the confusion?
2. As Jesse notes, theirs is a "50–50 partnership." Does it seem that way in how they interact? What is the power dynamic?

# Season 5, Episode 6: "Buyout"

Jesse and Mike (a later addition to the business) want out of the business, and have an opportunity to sell their share of the stolen chemicals. Jesse, who does not visit Walt in his "other" life, is invited over to Walt's house to discuss the opportunity.

This scene is a continuation of the discussion of the buyout offer. In the middle of the conversation, Skylar, Walt's wife, arrives home. She has just visited with her sister and has discovered that Walt told her sister about an affair she had within the past year.

This scene can be divided into two parts. The first half looks at the relationship between Jesse and Walt, Jesse's attempts at persuasion, and Walt's emotional reaction. The second half of the scene watches the communication dynamic change dramatically with the entrance of Skylar.

**Central Concepts:** Communication Climate, Conflict, Relational Dynamics
**Related Concepts**: Self-disclosure, Nonverbal Communication
**Length and Location of Scene 1**: Exactly 9 minutes (0:28:10–0:37:10)
**Opening Line**: (Walt opens the door.) "Yo, you sure this is OK?"
**Closing Line**: " . . . and you want to take it away from me."

**Discussion Questions**
1. How did Walt use self-disclosure in his conversation with Jesse?
2. How did Walt's and Jesse's communication patterns change from when they were alone to having Skylar present?
3. What relational messages were being sent at the dinner table?

# *HOUSE OF CARDS*

| *TV Show Data* | |
|---|---|
| Year Began | 2013 |
| Number of Seasons | 3 |
| Creator(s) | Beau Willimon |
| Genre | Political Drama |
| Episode Length | 55 Minutes |

| *Main Cast* | |
|---|---|
| **Character** | **Actor** |
| Francis Underwood | Kevin Spacey |
| Clair Underwood | Robin Wright |
| Doug Stamper | Michael Kelly |
| Zoe Barnes | Kate Mara |

### *TV Show Storyline*

*House of Cards* is known for having a dedicated following. The show begins with Congressman Frank Underwood celebrating in the aftermath of a presidential election, having helped the candidate win the election. Though promised nomination as Secretary of State, the new administration instead asks Frank to stay in Congress to help them move forward their legislative agenda. Although Frank agrees to support the President, he is angry about the snub and begins his own plans to move into increasingly more powerful positions.

**Note: This series contains strong language.**

**Note: The location of each scene is based on viewing the episode without commercials (e.g., Amazon Instant Video, Hulu Plus, iTunes, Netflix). Each episode is approximately 47 minutes in length.**

## Season 1, Episode 1: "Chapter 1"

In this first scene for analysis, we see Frank and Clair interact after Frank had been avoiding Clair's calls. This is directly after Frank met with the new President's chief of staff, and was told he wouldn't be getting the Secretary of State nomination.

**Central Concept**: Conflict
**Related Concepts**: Relational Messages, Emotional Expression
**Length and Location of Scene 1**: Approximately 2 minutes (0:13:45–0:15:35)
**Opening Line**: "Clair. . . ."
**Closing Line**: "My husband doesn't apologize, even to me."

**Discussion Questions**
1. How are Frank and Clair expressing their emotions about the situation?
2. What disconfirming messages do we see them use?
3. What is the source of this conflict? What conflict style do they use?

## Season 1, Episode 4: "Chapter 4"

In this scene, Clair and Frank discuss the possibility of a major donation to Clair's company. Clair is excited about the prospect of hiring back staff she had to fire after her company lost a donation when Frank wasn't nominated for Secretary of State and about the possibility of expanding the mission of her company. Frank is suspicious about the source of the donation.

**Central Concepts**: Conflict
**Related Concepts**: Power
**Length and Location of Scene 2**: Approximately 1 minute and 30 seconds (0:08:25–0:09:55)
**Opening Line**: "Hey . . . ."
**Closing Line**: "I'll tell you what I told him—I'll think about it."

**Discussion Questions**
1. How does this interaction reflect the definition of interpersonal conflict?
2. Who holds the power in this relationship? How do they attempt to exert power over one another?

# MAD MEN

| TV Show Data | |
|---|---|
| Year Began | 2007 |
| Number of Seasons | 7 |
| Creator(s) | Matthew Weiner |
| Genre | Period Drama |
| Episode Length | 47 Minutes |

| Main Cast | |
|---|---|
| **Character** | **Actor** |
| Donald "Don" Draper | Jon Hamm |
| Peter "Pete" Campbell | Vincent Kartheiser |
| Joan P. Harris | Christina Hendricks |
| Roger H. Sterling Jr. | John Slattery |
| Elizabeth "Betty" Draper | January Jones |
| Megan Draper | Jessica Paré |
| Margaret "Peggy" Olson | Elisabeth Moss |
| Sally Beth Draper | Kiernan Shipka |

## TV Show Storyline

*Mad Men* has garnered not only awards and critical acclaim but the public's fascination, for its historical authenticity, acting, writing, directing, costume and set design, and visual style. The show concentrates on the lives of a multitude of individuals living in the turbulent 1960s, ranging from female secretaries, to ad men, to children. Don Draper is the show's main character, and the audience quickly becomes well-acquainted with him and his wife (Betty) and daughter (Sally). However, there are many other ancillary characters that, as the seasons progress, become main characters themselves—for example, the social climbing secretary-turned-creative force Peggy Olson; or the stereotypical 1960s account man Pete Campbell, whose depth and complexity increase as his life unravels; or Don's daughter who comes of age amid her parents crumbling marriage. *Mad Men* becomes a landscape, littered with people and their daily struggles, both big and small.

**Note: The location of each scene is based on viewing the episode without commercials (e.g., Amazon Instant Video, Hulu Plus, iTunes, Netflix). Each episode is approximately 47 minutes in length.**

### Season 3, Episode 11: "The Gypsy and the Hobo"

In this first scene for analysis, Betty has uncovered the truth about Don's identity (that he was originally Richard Whitman). In the midst of one of his affairs, Don comes home to quickly change, only to be confronted by Betty regarding documents she found in his desk. Don is choked with emotion, but proceeds to tell her about his mysterious past, involving the real Donald Draper and the Korean War. Her reaction, coupled with Don's response, provides perfect fodder for concepts such as self-disclosure and identity management. This interchange is followed by a tenuous reconciliation between the two, as the episode ends with the entire family together, trick-or-treating.

**Central Concepts**: Self-Disclosure, Self-Concept/Identity Management
**Related Concepts**: Conflict, Family Communication, Honesty/Lying/Deception/Ethics, Nonverbal Communication, Relational Intimacy
**Length and Location of Scene 1**: Approximately 3½ minutes (0:27:33–0:31:02)
**Opening Line**: "The pictures covered with other people's names?"
**Closing Line**: "Donald Draper."

**Discussion Questions**
1. Why is Don so averse to disclosing his true identity to Betty, his wife? What does this say about his relationship with her?
2. When Betty asks Don who he is, why does Don say "Donald Draper" initially?
3. Identify the different types of nonverbal communication shown in this scene.

**Length and Location of Scene 2**: Approximately 1 minute and 15 seconds (0:45:26–0:46:38)
**Opening Line**: "Do I look like a gypsy?"
**Closing Line**: "And who are you supposed to be?"

**Discussion Questions**
1. What does Don and Betty's interaction before they go outside say about marriage/relationships in the 1960s? What is the subtext of Don's saying "good"?
2. Describe the family dynamics in this scene. How do Don and Betty express themselves to each other? To the children? How do these interactions compare to those of your family?
3. Analyze the final line of the scene. What is the subtext of Carlton's question? Would you be able to answer this question?

### Season 5, Episode 11: "The Other Woman"

The following two scenes are extremely interconnected in the context of the episode's narrative, which makes them exceptionally complementary. In the first scene for analysis, Pete approaches Joan with a salacious proposition. He suggests that she sleep with Herb Rennet, in order to win the Jaguar account. Joan is disgusted, yet Pete has planted the idea in her head. The second scene for analysis depicts Don pitching an idea to Herb and his partners. The entirety of his presentation is spliced with scenes of Joan following through with Pete's earlier request.

**Note: The start time for the second scene was chosen so as to avoid the scene with suggested sexual content involving Joan and Herb. There is no nudity in this scene, and it is up to the instructor whether or not to screen Don's full presentation.**

**Central Concepts:** Organizational Communication, Persuasion
**Related Concepts**: Conflict, Culture, Ethos/Pathos/Logos, Public Speaking, Gender and Sex Roles
**Length and Location of Scene 1**: Approximately 2½ minutes (0:05:33–0:08:06)
**Opening Line**: "You're here early."
**Closing Line**: "I understand."

**Discussion Questions**
1. How does Pete's position within the ad agency (an account man) affect his communicative behaviors, especially when propositioning Joan? Is there an interrelatedness of organizational experiences?
2. Discuss the interrelated power relationships within this scene. How much is this relationship informed by the culture of the 1960s, pertaining specifically to gender and sex roles?

**Length and Location of Scene 2**: Approximately 45 seconds (0:32:54–0:33:27)
**Opening Line**: "This thing."
**Closing Line**: No dialogue. Pete looks over at Herb.

**Discussion Questions**
1. How does Don go about persuading Herb and the other gentleman from Jaguar? Which rhetorical devices does he employ, and why are they effective?
2. Examine Don's public speaking. What is it about the way he presents that makes him so successful?
3. Choose a product, and attempt to persuade the class to buy it. Examine the angle(s) you used to persuade your classmates.

# MADAM SECRETARY

## TV Show Data

| | |
|---|---|
| Year Began | 2014 |
| Number of Seasons | 3 |
| Creator(s) | Barbara Hall |
| Genre | Drama |
| Episode Length | 43 minutes |

## Main Cast

| Character | Actor |
|---|---|
| Elizabeth McCord | Téa Leoni |
| Henry McCord | Tim Daly |
| Daisy Grant | Patina Miller |
| Matt Mahoney | Geoffrey Arend |
| Blake Moran | Erich Bergen |
| Alison McCord | Kathrine Herzer |
| Jason McCord | Evan Roe |
| Russell Jackson | Željko Ivanek |
| Nadine Tolliver | Bebe Neuwirth |
| Stephanie 'Stevie' McCord | Wallis Currie-Wood |
| President Conrad Dalton | Keith Carradine |
| Jay Whitman | Sebastian Arcelus |

## TV Show Storyline

Madam Secretary is a contemporary political drama focusing on the life and work of the Secretary of State, Elizabeth McCord. A graduate of the University of Virginia, McCord worked as a CIA analyst for some 20 years before becoming a professor of political science at her alma mater. Following what was subsequently revealed to be the suspicious death of her predecessor, President Conrad Dalton, McCord's former mentor in the CIA, asks her to head up the State Department. The President views her intellect, lateral thinking ability, knowledge of international affairs, and foreign language skills as particularly valuable for this position. He understands and even values her independence but also perceives her as a team player who respects his leadership. As Secretary of State, McCord sticks with the team she inherited, seeking help as might be needed from other trusted advisors, including her husband, Henry, a professor of theology at Georgetown University and himself a former NSA employee.

The show addresses a wide range of hot topics in today's political world, providing perhaps the most sophisticated analysis of political life in the executive branch and within a cabinet-level department yet to air on television. The Secretary's interactions and negotiations with an international set of political players in potential crisis situations provide intense dramatic story arcs in most episodes. Yet home life also remains a focus as Elizabeth juggles the demands of the White House and those of her three highly intelligent and often challenging children (born in the range from 1994 to 2001).

**Note: The location of each scene is based on viewing the episode without commercials (e.g., Netflix, Hulu Plus, iTunes). Each episode is approximately 43 minutes in length.**

## *Season 2, Episode 12: "The Middle Way"*

Three different but related storylines make up this episode. Elizabeth travels to Myanmar to finalize a multinational trade agreement that, among other things, will modernize the country's power grid using hydroelectricity. An unwelcome surprise awaits, however, in the form of U.S. Ambassador Arlen Maxwell, who has apparently gone native—in this case, Buddhist. In direct opposition to the American government he represents, Arlen renounces the deal, worried that it will displace whole villages of people in rural Myanmar. After inciting a peaceful demonstration outside the embassy, the increasingly desperate ambassador takes the President of Myanmar hostage at his palace, violating his pacifist Buddhist principles. Nadine Tolliver, Elizabeth's chief of staff, has decided to accompany her on this diplomatic mission for largely personal reasons, hoping to reestablish contact with her estranged son, who is living in Myanmar. On the home front, Henry, aided by Blake, is left to host a meeting of neighbors hostile to the changes brought about by the presence of Elizabeth's secret service detail on the street and other problems associated with living next door to the highest-ranking Cabinet official.

**Central Concept**: Conflict
**Related Concept**: Communication Climate, Escalatory Spiral
**Length and Location of Scene 1**: Approximately 1 minute (17 minutes into episode)
**Opening Line**: "Mr. President, thank you for seeing me."
**Closing Line**: "Everybody out or the President dies."
**Length and Location of Scene 2**: Approximately 4 minutes (22 minutes into episode)
**Opening Line:** "Sergio and Alice, three doors down."
**Closing Line:** "Great diplomacy, guys. Really top-notch."
**Length and Location of Scene 3**: Approximately 6 minutes (31 minutes into episode)
**Opening Line:** "Oh, it's okay. Thank you."
**Closing Line:** "Well, there's only one way to find out."

**Discussion Questions**

1. In Scene 1, the President of Myanmar reminds Ambassador Arlen of another Buddhist Noble Truth: "Don't struggle to get what you want but modify your wanting." Arlen clearly rejects this counsel, opting instead to take the President hostage at gunpoint. Drawing on communication theory, compare and contrast these two styles of conflict resolution. Consider cultural influences in your explanation.

2. In Scene 2, the communication climate quickly degenerates at what promised initially to be a successful neighborhood gathering hosted by Henry and Blake. How did the reciprocal pattern of communication among the group produce a negative escalatory spiral? What did Henry and Blake do right, and what did they do wrong in this exercise in conflict management?

3. In Scene 3, we learn about how Nadine managed conflict with her son in the past. Compare this style to the new tactic she decides to adopt here. How does a decision to just "suck-it-up" figure in conflict theory, and how does this approach inspire Madam Secretary's epiphany, one that allows her to successfully renegotiate the contentious treaty in Myanmar?

4. In what ways might Henry and Elizabeth take "the middle way" to resolve the dispute with their neighbors?

## *Season 2, Episode 14: "Left of the Boom"*

Elizabeth begins the day looking forward to personally hosting a D.C. conference, whose keynote speaker is a 20-year-old Saudi advocate for women's equality in education and the workplace, activist efforts for which she gained international fame and suffered a disfiguring acid attack. Elizabeth is subsequently called to the Oval Office, however, along with the male directors of the CIA and an FBI unit responsible for the nation's cybersecurity. The President chastises the two directors for their lapses in what is believed to be a breach initiated by the Chinese. Elizabeth offers to seek out a Chinese contact who has proved useful in the past to assess China's culpability. She is more interested, though, in pursuing the theft of a supply of uranium in Moldova. The directors downplay the uranium theft, but Elizabeth secures the President's permission to follow up and take the lead on these matters with the assistance of the other intelligence units. She is also concerned about two American girls who ran off to join a Muslim terrorist group in Libya but were arrested by the Saudi government, a fact she discovers in an unexpected visit from the deputy director of the counterterrorism unit of the FBI, Marguerite Sanchez. On the home front, Henry learns at a parent–teacher conference that Alison's grades are fine, but she has been implicated in a social media incident at the school.

**Central Concept**: Gender
**Related Concept**: Problem Solving, Conflict Resolution, Social Media
**Length and Location of Scene 1**: Approximately 4 minutes (3 minutes into episode)
**Opening Line**: "You're telling me DOD and Cybercom, the entire intelligence community, none of you could stop China from stealing a key piece of our defense?
**Closing Line**: "Gently, please."

## Discussion Questions

1. Describe the variety of communication styles apparent in these interactions at the White House. Do they support or challenge the research on gender and communication? Consider gendered approaches to problem solving and conflict management in addition to use of language.

2. In a later scene (11 minutes into the episode), Marguerite Sanchez, FBI Deputy Director of Counterterrorism expresses her hope that it wasn't inappropriate for her to have contacted Madame Secretary, who replies, "Of course. I wish more of us reached out. You think it's a departmental thing or a guy thing? That's okay. Don't answer that." If you were encouraged to answer that question, how would you respond?

3. Malala Yousafzai, a Pakistani activist for female education and the youngest person to win the Nobel Prize, clearly inspired this episode that features a fictional Saudi advocate instead. Describe some of the restrictions on the communication and behavior of women in these countries. Should citizens of Western countries be committed to promoting global equality for women in these and similar nations?

**Length and Location of Scene 2**: Approximately 1 minute (14 minutes into episode)
**Opening Line**: "She's doing great. Her math scores are up."
**Closing Line**: "Yes. Full religion professor. Go."

## Discussion Questions

1. While acknowledging things could be worse, Elizabeth is still upset by her daughter's apparent behavior on social media. Does Alison's comment constitute cyberbullying? Why or why not? We learn later that someone else posted this comment in Alison's name, yet Alison, concerned for her popularity with the in-group, did nothing to correct this misattribution. How would you assess her non-response?

2. Elizabeth describes this instance of social media behavior as "mean-girl crap." Are there gender differences in how the sexes communicate meanness? If so, do differences vary with communication medium?

# MODERN FAMILY

## TV Show Data

| | |
|---|---|
| Year Began | 2009 |
| Number of Seasons | 7 |
| Creator(s) | Steve Levitan, Christopher Lloyd |
| Genre | Situation Comedy |
| Episode Length | 30 minutes |

## Main Cast

| Character | Actor |
|---|---|
| Jay Pritchett | Ed O'Neill |
| Gloria Delgado-Pritchett | Sofia Vergara |
| Claire Dunphy | Julie Bowen |
| Phil Dunphy | Ty Burrell |
| Mitchell Pritchett | Jesse Tyler Ferguson |
| Cameron Tucker | Eric Stonestreet |
| Manny Delgado | Rico Rodriguez |
| Luke Dunphy | Nolan Gould |
| Haley Dunphy | Ariel Winter |

### TV Show Storyline

If you have turned on your television recently, or watched popular TV shows online, then you are likely familiar with the situation comedy *Modern Family*. As the title suggests, the show is a collection of characters comprising a variety of family types. There is the more traditional family unit, consisting of husband Phil Dunphy, his wife Claire, and their children Haley, Alex, and Luke. There's also Mitchell (Claire's biological brother) and Cameron, two gay men who have an adopted child from Vietnam. Lastly, there's the patriarch of the entire show: Jay (biological father of Claire and Mitchell). Jay is divorced and remarried to a much younger woman, Gloria, who has a young son named Manny.

Most episode plots involve issues relevant to raising children, such as sibling rivalries, parental decisions, and family conflict. Other storylines range from the mundane (what to wear on the first day of school) to the unusual (where to go for the family trip). The show is also shot in pseudo-documentary style, which allows the storylines to play out accompanied by the characters' analyses and confessions made directly to the camera. Not only do these moments make for humorous commentary, they also serve as examples of metacommunication.

**Note: The location of each scene is based on viewing the episode without commercials (e.g., Amazon Instant Video, Hulu Plus, iTunes). Each episode is approximately 22 minutes in length.**

## *Season 2, Episode 5: "Unplugged"*

In this episode, Claire is fed up with her family's addiction to technology (e.g., cell phones, video games, and computers). In order to cure them of their affliction, Claire and Phil attempt a bold idea: no technology for anyone for an entire week, and whoever can go the longest without technology wins a prize. Soon enough the family members, including Phil and Claire, struggle to wean themselves of life's little electronic conveniences. It's anyone's guess who can hold out the longest.

**Central Concept**: Technology
**Related Concepts**: Computer-Mediated Communication
**Length and Location of Scene 1**: Approximately 2 minutes (0:01:20–0:03:10)
**Opening Line**: "Okay, there you go."
**Closing Line**: "That's awesome."

**Discussion Questions**
1. Is the Dunphys' use of technology typical of most families today? Provide examples.
2. Claire exclaims that families are "supposed to talk" without technology. Does technology isolate family members from each other, or does technology bring them closer together? Please explain with examples.

**Length and Location of Scene 2**: Approximately 2 minutes (0:04:30–0:06:10)
**Opening Line**: "Okay, we have called this family meeting because the personal electronics have gotten out of control."
**Closing Line**: "I have almost no faith in you."

**Discussion Questions**
1. How dependent are you on technology?
2. Would it be possible for you to completely unplug from technology for more than a few days? Please explain.

**Note: There are more scenes in this episode that close the Dunphy storyline on technology. These scenes were not mentioned here, mostly because they are humorous but offer little additional content for analysis.**

## *Season 2, Episode 17: "Two Monkeys and a Panda"*

This episode presents a so-called typical day for the Dunphy family—typical, at least, for Claire. Notably, se while Claire is driving all over town running errands and trying to solve family crises, Phil is getting a make-over at a local beauty spa. Exasperated and practically at her wit's end, Claire telephones Phil and asks him to make dinner that night. Their conversation does not end well, and Phil is left bewildered about what went wrong. Fortunately for him, Phil just happens to be surrounded by a group of women who are more than willing to teach him the differences between male and female communication.

**Central Concept**: Gender
**Related Concepts**: Supportive Communication, Listening, Communication Climate
**Length and Location of Scene 1**: Approximately 1 minute (0:08:18–0:09:25)
**Opening Line**: "I'm thinking of getting bangs."
**Closing Line**: "Hello? What?"

### Discussion Questions
1. How would you describe Phil's style of talk? What is the goal of communication for Phil? Is his style typical of men? Please explain.
2. Place yourself in Claire's position. Why is she so upset after talking with Phil? How would you label Phil's listening style?
3. Explain how Phil should have spoken to Claire, focusing on gender styles and communication expectations.

**Length and Location of Scene 2**: Approximately 1½ minutes (0:12:30–0:13:54)
**Opening Line**: "Okay, I'm confused."
**Closing Line**: "Okay, now I'm confused again."

### Discussion Questions
1. Do you agree or disagree with the advice these women gave to Phil? Why?
2. Do you agree or disagree with their analysis of female expectations for communication? Why?

**Length and Location of Scene 3**: Approximately 2 minutes (0:15:30–0:17:40)
**Opening Line**: "Is she back yet!?"
**Closing Line**: "I'll just go make dinner."

### Discussion Questions
1. Evaluate Phil's style of talk now. Was he able to provide supportive communication for Claire? Please explain.
2. How would you label Phil's listening style now?

## Season 3, Episode 13: "Little Bo Bleep"

One storyline in this episode centers on Claire running for City Council. The episode begins with a recent article in the local newspaper reporting that "Claire Dunphy is angry and unlikable." In order to improve her image and prepare for the election, Phil and the children suggest having a mock debate. That way, Claire can practice her talking points about the issues and polish her delivery skills. Additionally, her family can also point out all of her negative nonverbal cues. As you watch this scene, try to identify the different types of nonverbal cues that Claire exhibits. Is her family's criticism justified? When making a first impression, does nonverbal communication make that much of a difference?

**Central Concepts**: Nonverbal Communication
**Related Concepts**: Public Speaking
**Length and Location of Scene**: Approximately 3 minutes (0:04:35–0:07:25)
**Opening Line**: "Welcome, candidates."
**Closing Line**: *"She's ready."*

**Discussion Questions**
1. Identify the different functions of nonverbal communication (e.g., repeating, substituting, complementing, accenting, regulating, and contradicting) that Claire displays.
2. Label the types of nonverbal cues (kinesics, haptics, proxemics, etc.) that Claire displays.
3. Do you agree that nonverbal communication affects the perceptions of a political candidate's image or credibility? Recall and discuss an actual example when a politician's nonverbal communication influenced his or her credibility—either positively or negatively.

A second storyline in this episode, and a helpful bridge between nonverbal and verbal communication, concerns the use of inappropriate language. It seems that Lily, the young daughter of Mitchell and Cameron, has picked up on a certain swear word. When Lily drops the F-bomb in front of her parents, Mitchell is aghast while Cameron can barely contain his laughter. However, they are both concerned that Lily will embarrass them in public at an upcoming wedding, where Lily will be the flower girl. How do we learn language? And why do we seem to learn the inappropriate words first? Is Mitchell overreacting, or is Cameron out of touch with the seriousness of this issue?

**Central Concepts**: Language
**Related Concepts**: Rules of Language, Swearing
**Length and Location of Scene 1**: Approximately 1 minute (0:07:25–0:08:40)
**Opening Line**: "And it's this."
**Closing Line**: "I have two children."

**Discussion Questions**
1. Which rules of language (phonetic, syntactic, semantic, or pragmatic) are demonstrated in this scene?
2. Have you ever witnessed a young child swearing? What was your reaction?
3. Do you agree with Mitchell that Lily should be told this is a bad word, or do you side with Cameron's advice to ignore the issue? Why?

**Length and Location of Scene 2**: Approximately 1 minute (0:11:15–0:12:30)
**Opening Line**: "Do you have any idea what station this is on?"
**Closing Line**: "We leave town on Gay Pride weekend because we don't like the traffic."

**Discussion Questions**
1. What is Lily's reason for using this word? What does this suggest about her understanding of language and meanings?
2. What is your opinion about adults using swear words? Is swearing ever okay? What about at home or with friends? In the workplace? Have you ever had a teacher swear in class? Was it appropriate or inappropriate? Why?

## *Season 3, Episode 14: "Me? Jealous?"*

This episode begins with Phil and Claire entertaining a top real-estate agent (Tad, played by Greg Kinnear). Ultimately, Phil wants to join Tad's firm, since this should give Phil more access to higher-end properties on the market. Dinner with Tad goes well until he starts to leave, and he plants a firm kiss on Claire's lips. Surprisingly, Phil does not notice Tad's kiss. What follows is a humorous example of nonverbal expectancies, and the possible reactions when those expectancies are violated by someone else.

**Central Concept**: Nonverbal Communication
**Related Concepts**: Expectancy Violations, Regulative and Constitutive Rules, Jealousy
**Length and Location of Scene 1**: Approximately 2½ minutes (0:02:05–0:03:45)
**Opening Line**: "Tad, this wine is fantastic."
**Closing Line**: "It's a progressive culture. Most of them travel by zip-line."

**Discussion Questions**
1. Given the context of the situation and the relationship between the characters, why is Tad's nonverbal communication unexpected for Claire?
2. Why is Phil blind to Tad's behavior?

**Length and Location of Scene 2**: Approximately 2 minutes (0:08:05–0:09:45)
**Opening Line**: "Honey, I'm home."
**Closing Line**: "Do you realize how insulting that is?"

**Discussion Questions**
1. After watching this second scene, now speculate why Phil is still blind to Tad's behavior. Use expectancy violations to explain your answer.
2. Describe a situation in which your perception of nonverbal communication was very different from someone else's perception. Why were these different perceptions present?

**Length and Location of Scene 3**: Approximately 3 minutes (0:18:05–0:20:40)
**Opening Line**: "Have a seat."
**Closing Line**: "I'd like to go back."

**Discussion Questions**
1. Use regulative and constitutive rules to explain Phil's reasons for leaving Tad's house.
2. For Claire, Phil's jealousy is a sign that he cares about her. In that way, could partner jealousy be a good thing? Why or why not?

# ORANGE IS THE NEW BLACK

### TV Show Data

| Year Began | 2013 |
|---|---|
| Number of Seasons | 3 |
| Creator(s) | Jenji Kohan |
| Genre | Comedy, Crime, Drama |
| Episode Length | 55 minutes |

### Main Cast

| Character | Actor |
|---|---|
| Piper Chapman | Taylor Schilling |
| Alex Vause | Laura Prepon |
| Sam Healy | Michael J. Harney |
| Miss Claudette Pelage | Michelle Hurst |
| Galina "Red" Reznikov | Kate Mulgrew |
| Larry Bloom | Jason Biggs |
| Suzanne "Crazy Eyes" Warren | Uzo Aduba |
| Tasha "Taystee" Jefferson | Danielle Brooks |
| Nicole "Nicky" Nichols | Natasha Lyonne |

### TV Show Storyline

Based on Piper Kerman's memoir *Orange Is the New Black: My Year in a Women's Prison*, the series follows Piper Chapman, an upper middle class yuppie from New York who is sentenced to 15 months in federal prison for transporting drug money for her ex-girlfriend Alex Vause (Laura Prepon). A decade after she commits the crime and two years before the statute of limitations on it runs out, Piper is thrust into prison life and a forced reunion with Alex.

## Season 1, Episode 1: "I Wasn't Ready"

The pilot episode revolves around the protagonist's first days in prison and introduces a colorful cast of characters, from correctional officer Sam Healy (Michael J. Harney), who sees Piper as a welcome addition to the ward, to warmhearted yet tempestuous prison cook Red (Kate Mulgrew). Scenes showing Piper's all-but-smooth transition into prison life are interspersed with flashbacks from her former one, revealing stark contrasts and the story behind her decade-old offense.

**Central Concept**: Culture Shock
**Related Concepts**: Expectancy Violation, Proxemics
**Length and Location of Scene**: Approximately 2 minutes (0:00:01–0:002:00)
**Opening Line**: "I've always loved getting clean."
**Closing Line**: "*[Singing]* Ain't nobody crying . . . Ain't nobody worried."

### Discussion Questions
1. Describe Piper's experience of culture shock, including her loss of personal space. How does she adapt to her new circumstances?
2. Identify how violations of expectations are demonstrated in this scene. Is the loss of privacy an entirely negative violation for Piper?
3. Have you ever experienced culture shock, or a feeling of disorientation in a new and unfamiliar environment? Describe the situation and how you felt. Looking back, what did you learn to help you navigate similar situations in the future?

## Season 1, Episode 6: "The WAC Pack"

In this episode, a scuffle over the television results in the revival of the women's advisory council, which is to be composed of one representative from each ethnicity. In anticipation of the election, the inmates campaign for spots and engage in a rap battle for dominance.

**Central Concept**: Perception (Stereotyping and Prejudice)
**Related Concepts**: Identity, Culture
**Length and Location of Scene**: Approximately 4 minutes and 30 seconds (0:17:05–0:21:35)
**Opening Line**: "So I'm thinking campaign posters instead of buttons."
**Closing Line**: "Quiet down!"

### Discussion Questions
1. Discuss the role that perception and stereotyping play in this scene. In what ways do the characters engage in stereotyping?
2. What is the basis for the group stereotypes illustrated here? Are they persistent? Are they warranted?
3. How does being part of a cultural or ethnic group influence your identity?

# *SPEECHLESS*

| TV Show Data | |
|---|---|
| Year Began | 2016 |
| Number of Seasons | 1 |
| Creator(s) | Scott Silveri |
| Genre | Situation Comedy |
| Episode Length | 22 minutes |

| Main Cast | |
|---|---|
| **Character** | **Actor** |
| Maya Dimeo | Minnie Driver |
| Jimmy Dimeo | John Ross Bowie |
| Kenneth | Cedric Yarbrough |
| Ray Dimeo | Mason Cook |
| JJ DiMeo | Micah Fowler |
| Dylan DiMeo | Kyla Kennedy |
| Jillian | Lukita Maxwell |

## TV Show Storyline

The series begins as Maya DiMeo is relocating her husband and three children yet again in the hope that a better school district will provide better opportunities for her high-spirited and witty teenage son with cerebral palsy. A fiercely protective mother, Maya crusades to ensure that her special needs son enjoys the significant activities that his peers take for granted, well-intentioned campaigns that tend to have unintended consequences. The principal of Lafayette High School, for her part, embraces standards of diversity and inclusivity but is typically challenged by their application. And JJ's new aide, whom he has unexpectedly plucked from his job as high school janitor, operates largely from instinct rather than specialized knowledge or expertise.

Eager for new experiences, JJ, the oldest of the three DiMeo children, is excited about the new high school, where for the first time he has a companion/caretaker, who aids and abets him in his innovative quest to overcome communication and mobility challenges. Serious, sensitive, and studious Ray, the middle child, is often critical of his family's eccentricities and embarrassing deviations from the norm, while younger sister Dylan remains thick skinned and brutally honest, a jock who shoots straight from the hip. In its frank and heartening depiction of a multi-faceted special-needs family, *Speechless* celebrates strength in diversity on various dimensions.

**Note: The location of each scene is based on viewing the episode without commercials (e.g., Amazon Instant Video, Hulu Plus, iTunes). Each episode is approximately 22 minutes in length.**

## *Season 1, Episode 3: "B-O-N—BONFIRE"*

Adding idioms like "What's up" and pop culture references such as "Kanye," Maya updates JJ's board to make his language options more hip. Well-intentioned changes on her son's behalf don't end there, though, as she focuses her transformative energies once again on Lafayette High School, specifically, its annual homecoming celebration that culminates in a student bonfire on the beach. Thinking solely of JJ's disappointment at being excluded because the location is wheelchair inaccessible, Maya lobbies successfully to have the event canceled. The annual beach bonfire, with neither a beach nor a bonfire, is held instead at the school gym, where students end up voicing their disappointment and disapproval in a rap session proposed by the principal. JJ, who was becoming popular with the in-crowd at school, is equally unhappy with his mom. Elsewhere, Jimmy tries to help Ray with his love life by decluttering the house of the junk their family is wont to accumulate. Yet father and son soon discover that collecting other people's stuff is a difficult habit for them to break. These two separate storylines are presented in short alternating segments listed here as one scene.

**Central Concept**: Diversity
**Related Concept**: Persuasion, Perspective taking, Reflected Appraisal
**Scene Length and Location**: Approximately 6 minutes (0:10:35–0:16:45)
**Opening Line**: "Welcome to the new, improved inclusive homecoming bonfire."
**Closing Line**: "I got it dad. I'm bulletproof too."

**Discussion Questions**
1. When the principal says, "I'm sensing a lot of unspoken thoughts," what types of non-verbal communication is she referring to? Describe how attendees convey their dissatisfaction with the "new improved inclusive bonfire" without saying a word.
2. The rap session led by the principal violates certain communication rules for this type of conversational forum while maintaining others. Which norms do participants observe, and which do they flout, and with what results? Transgressions occur here with comic effect, but how would you have felt about this discussion if you had actually been there?
3. Of the people who spoke out during the rap session, who did you find most persuasive, and why? Consider their appeals to pathos, logos, and ethos.
4. Ray's self-esteem suffers because he fears negative reflected appraisal. Specifically, he, like many teenagers, is concerned that others do not view him and his family as normal. What is Jimmy's opinion of the opinion of others? Explain how he uses perspective taking to persuade his son that "normal" is not necessarily ideal.

## *Season 1, Episode 8: "T-H-A—THANKSGIVING"*

In this holiday episode, the DiMeos attempt to get out of Thanksgiving dinner with Jimmy's brother at his country club, an annual event they all dread with, as we discover, good reason. Their cover story about JJ being ill fails, however, when Billy and family decide to travel to the

DiMeos' house for dinner, where the family (minus sensible and sensitive Ray) has decided to amuse themselves with an arguably mean-spirited parlor game. This year they will keep a clandestine running tally of their relatives' annoying habits and declare the DiMeo who has had to endure the most vexation the winner. When Kenneth asks what they find so objectionable, the litany is comprehensive: Wife Audrey weeps at the least provocation and talks to J.J. like he is deaf. Mother-in-law corners J.J to perform her latest dance routine. Son Duncan restricts his conversation to mindless repetition of his latest catchphrase. Brother Billy brags boorishly without end and with apparent delight at showing his brother up. Naturally, the DiMeo deception is exposed, but using honest dialogue that helps heal longstanding interpersonal conflicts ensues, they manage to salvage the holiday and familial relationships.

**Central Concept**: Deception
**Related Concept**: Ethics, Communication Competence
**Length and Location of Scene 1**: 4:30 minutes (0:01:45–0:6:15)
**Opening Line**: "Kenneth, Jimmy and I were just talking. We decided to stay home for Thanksgiving."
**Closing Line**: "Now that's something to be thankful for. Noish [sic]."

**Discussion Questions**
1. What kinds of lies does the family consider using and then eventually decide on to avoid the annual Thanksgiving dinner? Is this "get-out-of-jail-free card" ethical? Of these three categories—altruistic lies, self-serving lies, and evasions—which is most likely to have serious consequences for relationships?
2. Consider when you have lied to get out of an unpleasant event. What were the consequences? Situational ethics considers context when evaluating behavior. When do you feel deception is justified?
3. How does the deception the DiMeos have planned for their relatives on Thanksgiving differ from the lie they told them in an effort to avoid this get-together? Is this deception justified by the particular circumstances?

**Length and Location of Scene 2**: 1:40 minutes (0:08:40–0:10:20)
**Opening Line**: "And here's the bathroom."
**Closing Line**: "So things are good."

**Discussion Questions**
1. Describe how varied behaviors exhibited at the DiMeo's house on Thanksgiving demonstrate communication incompetence. Which of these behaviors have you witnessed most frequently, and which do you find most objectionable?
2. What is humblebragging? Cite a number of examples provided by Billy and from your own experience. Is humblebragging more or less annoying than bragging?
3. In which situations might it be necessary to speak of your achievements? How do you engage in self-promotion without becoming annoyingly boastful?

# STRANGER THINGS

### TV Show Data

| | |
|---|---|
| Year Began | 2016 |
| Number of Seasons | 2 |
| Creators | Matt Duffer, Ross Duffer |
| Genre | Science fiction, horror |
| Episode Length | 42–62 minutes |

### Main Cast

| Character | Actor |
|---|---|
| Joyce Byers | Winona Ryder |
| Jim Hopper | David Harbour |
| Mike Wheeler | Finn Wolfhard |
| Eleven | Millie Bobby Brown |
| Dustin Henderson | Gaten Matarazzo |
| Lucas Sinclair | Caleb McLaughlin |
| Nancy Wheeler | Natalia Dyer |
| Jonathan Byers | Charlie Heaton |
| Steve Harrington | Joe Keery |
| Dr. Martin Brenner | Matthew Modine |

### TV Show Storyline

Things are indeed getting stranger and stranger in 1983 in Hawkins, Indiana, where until recently the weirdest occurrence, according to the local sheriff, involved an owl that mistook Eleanor Gillespie's hair for its nest. Now a series of enigmatic abductions and murders have abruptly awakened the sleepy backwater to evil lurking in their midst. These horrors are presaged by the opening scene in which elevator doors close on a scientist as he is savaged by some unseen monster at the mysterious Hawkins National Laboratory. More significantly for the principal plot, a middle school boy (Will) goes missing, followed by the similarly ominous disappearance of a high school girl (Barbara). The entity responsible for these events is a predatory alien—a creature known only to the Hawkins scientists, whose highly classified government research focuses on both understanding this life form and exploiting the psychic and telekinetic abilities of a young girl (Eleven) who can communicate with it. Foiling these objectives, a deeply traumatized Eleven manages to flee this life of abusive captivity when she happens upon Will's buddies. With varying degrees of enthusiasm, they accept "El" in their tight-knit group as she redirects her psychic energy to avoid recapture, protect her new friends, and aid their search for Will.

# Season 1, Chapter 1: "The Vanishing of Will Byer"

In an opening scene, we are introduced to 12-year-old Will and his group of friends (Mike, Dustin, and Lucas) during their regular session of Dungeons and Dragons (D&D) at Mike's house. Biking home at night after the game, Will is abducted by his own Demagorgon, an alien creature he encounters on the road. The day following Will's disappearance, a young girl (Eleven) with a shaved head steals food from a local diner owned by Benny, whose anger at the theft is soon eclipsed by curiosity about and compassion for this visibly traumatized and famished child who appeared out of nowhere in a hospital gown. Their budding relationship is cut short, however, when Benny becomes collateral damage in the bad guys' first bid to recover Eleven. Meanwhile, Will's mother enlists a skeptical sheriff to search for her son, a quest that Will's friends are independently pursuing when they find Eleven hiding in the woods.

**Central Concepts**: Friendship, Gender
**Related Concepts**: Small-Group Communication, Gaming, Technology
**Length and Location of Scene 1**: Approximately 4 minutes (~ 0:01:40–0:5:31)
**Opening Line**: "Something is coming. Something hungry for blood."
**Closing Line**: "Son of a bitch."

**Discussion Questions**
1. This opening scene introduces the principal young protagonists while establishing their characteristic style of communication. Describe the interpersonal style of each friend in this small group.
2. How do the boys communicate friendship in this scene? Does their behavior exhibit gendered norms of communication? If so, how?
3. How are friendships created or maintained through the interaction that occurs during games? How do gendered norms of communication affect gameplay? Were groups of girls, for example, even likely to play D&D in 1983? How have gender demographics in gaming changed since then?
4. Dungeons and Dragons debuted in 1974, a pioneer (some argue the progenitor) in fantasy role-playing games (RPGs) whose enormous success launched an industry. In 2006, a massively multiplayer online role-playing game (MMORPG) of D&D was developed. From a communication perspective, how would technological innovation influence and distinguish these gaming experiences? Consider the pros and cons of interaction in the low-tech board game versus the high-tech online version.

**Central Concepts**: Gender, Language
**Related Concepts**: Content and Relational Messages, Escalatory Spiral
**Length and Location of Scene 2**: Approximately 2 minutes (~ 0:17:10–0:18:52)
**Opening Line**: "I've been waiting here for over an hour, Hopper."
**Closing Line**: "Just find my son, Hop. Find him."

**Discussion Questions**

1. This exchange between Joyce and Sheriff Hopper reveals that Will has apparently violated 1980s gender norms of masculinity in the eyes of some of his peers and his estranged father, Lonnie. Discuss masculine norms of communication and whether Will would be bullied or harassed for such perceived transgressions today.

2. "Queer" has a long and ugly history as a pejorative for non-heterosexuals, particularly gay men. More recently, members of the LGBT community reclaimed this as a self-affirming umbrella identifier, an effort that sparked some debate. Do you agree that "queer" can work as a positive, oppositional signifier in language, or do you believe that the continued use of this term, even among those in the LGBT community, perpetuates harmful stereotypes?

3. Describe the content and relational messages in the conversation between Sheriff Hopper and Joyce.

4. What is an escalatory spiral, and how was a negative spiral avoided in this conflict situation?

## *Season 1, Chapter 2: "The Weirdo on Maple Street"*

The boys decide to shelter Eleven at Mike's house, where she takes up clandestine residence in the basement. El, as nicknamed by Mike, reveals that "bad people" are after her, and with visceral concern presumably prompted by her history at the Hawkins Lab, she recognizes Will in one of Mike's photos. Meanwhile in another storyline of short scenes alternating with other story arcs, Nancy (Mike's sister) coerces Barb into going with her to a party at her boyfriend's house when his parents are out of town. Jonathan, investigating the nearby woods where his brother went missing, hears screaming, only to discover the high school group partying poolside. Jonathan photographs them secretly at a distance while Barb, alone outside after best friend Nancy dismisses her to join boyfriend Steve in his bedroom, vanishes.

**Central Concepts**: Friendship, Expectancy Violations
**Related Concepts**: Self-Disclosure, Gender, Confirming and Disconfirming Messages
**Length and Location of Scene 1**: Approximately 1 minute (~ 0:35:53–0:37:04)
**Opening Line**: "El? No adults. Just us and some meatloaf."
**Closing Line**: "That's super-important because friends tell each other things. Things that parents don't know."
**Length and Location of Scene 2**: Approximately 1 1/2 minutes (~ 0:37:10–0:38:32)
**Opening Line**: "Barbara. Pullover."
**Closing Line**: "Hello, Ladies."
**Length and Location of Scene 3**: Approximately 2 minutes (~ 0:43:00–0:45:00)
**Opening Line**: "You're such an asshole, Tommy."
**Closing Line**: "What the hell, Tommy?"
**Length and Location of Scene 4**: Approximately 1 minute (~ 0:49:20–0:50:14)
**Opening Line**: "Oh my god, I'm freezing."
**Closing Line**: "Just go ahead and go home, okay?"

**Discussion Questions**

1. How does Mike and the boys' definition of friendship compare to the criteria described in communication theory? To your personal definition? What role does self-disclosure play in friendship? Do children often refrain from sharing secrets with their parents, and with what possible consequences?

2. Identify the rules or expectations that govern communication in successful friendships. What expectancy violations has Nancy committed in her interaction with Barb? Does Nancy qualify as a friend according to her brother Mike's definition? How does Nancy's friendship with Barb compare to the friendships in the group of younger boys? Describe the gendered communication in Nancy and Barb's same-sex friendship.

3. Describe the kinds of confirming or disconfirming messages used to persuade Barb to behave in certain ways in these scenes. Have you ever found yourself in a situation where you felt coerced by a friend or by peer pressure? How did you respond?

## *Season 1, Chapter 4: "The Body"*

Joyce refuses to be persuaded that the body in the morgue is Will. Meanwhile back at Mike's home, El succeeds in contacting Will on Mike's walkie-talkie, proof of life for her new friends. Realizing the need for more powerful communication technology, the boys give El a gendered makeover so that she can pass as a girl pal at school, where they have access to Mr. Clarke's ham radio. An obstacle to their goal arises when Mr. Clarke insists the group attend a memorial for Will being held at the school gymnasium, where the school bullies' derogatory remarks about Will incense both Mike and El. As the students stream out after the assembly, Mike confronts the group's nemesis, Troy, a conflict in which El intervenes, giving the bully a taste of his own medicine spiked by the paranormal.

**Central Concepts**: Gender, Self-Concept, Bullying
**Related Concepts**: Perceived Self, Presenting Self, Reflected Appraisal
**Length and Location of Scene 1**: Approximately 1 1/2 minutes (0:17:20–0:18:50)
**Opening Line**: "This isn't gonna work. We need to get El to a stronger radio."
**Closing Line**: "Pretty. Good."
**Length and Location of Scene 2**: Approximately 2 minutes (0:29:20–0:31:30)
**Opening Line**: "I'd like to introduce you to Sandy Sloane."
**Closing Line**: "Mike. Let's go!"

**Discussion Questions**

1. Describe how the boys' makeover of El conveys their visual conception of femininity. How might El have been received at school had they allowed her to retain an androgynous style or dressed her in a less "girly" manner? How have gendered norms for clothing and appearance changed since the 1980s?

2. The boys have encountered an essentially blank slate in El, who entered 1980s society with no sense of its norms and little sense of herself in relation to conventions she finds utterly foreign. That said, describe El's self-concept—her perceived self, her presenting self, and the impact of reflected appraisal illustrated in this scene.

3. Describe the nature of the school bullies' verbal aggression in this scene. Many would consider public humiliation just payback for their serial abuse of Will and his group of friends. Do you think Mike was right to confront Troy as he did? Given El's lack of socialization and her own history of abuse at the lab, her response is understandable, even cheer-worthy from a dramatic perspective, but did her intervention go too far from a communication perspective?

# UNBREAKABLE KIMMY SCHMIDT

| TV Show Data | |
|---|---|
| Year Began | 2015 |
| Number of Seasons | 3 |
| Creator | Tina Fey, Robert Carlock |
| Genre | Sitcom |
| Episode Length | ~ 30 minutes |

| Main Cast | |
|---|---|
| Character | Actor |
| Kimmy Schmidt | Ellie Kemper |
| Titus Andromedon | Titus Burgess |
| Lillian Kaushtupper | Carol Kane |
| Jane Krakowski | Jacqueline Voorhees |
| Mike Carlsen | Mikey Politano |
| Xanthippe Voorhees | Dylan Gelula |
| Mimi Kanasis | Amy Sedaris |
| Perry | Daveed Diggs |
| Richard Wayne Gary Wayne | John Hamm |

*TV Show Storyline*

After being freed from an underground bunker in Indiana where she spent 15 years of captivity with a doomsday cult, Kimmy Schmidt is determined to make up for lost time and begin a happy, new chapter in New York City. Enduring a lifetime of abuse at the hands of the reverend who kidnapped her has only strengthened her resolve to rebuild her life as a survivor. She refuses to be broken by her past, reentering 1990s society with relentless and infectious good cheer. Cracks occasionally appear in her armor of optimism, though, posttraumatic stress disorder that takes varied forms including flatulence, flashbacks, nightmares, blackouts, and seemingly random episodes of lashing out. A cast of colorful characters both challenge and aid Kimmy's adjustment to life in the Big Apple. These include a hippie landlord (Lillian Kaushtauper), a gay roommate, (Titus Andromedon), a Manhattan socialite, (Jacqueline Voorhees), and an alcoholic therapist, (Dr. Andrea Bayden).

## Season 2, Episode 7: "Kimmy Walks into a Bar"

In the primary story arc, Jacqueline Voorhees needs to reinvent her seasonal gala when a scheduling error threatens to derail the event entirely. This series of brief scenes, however, follows Titus's developing relationship with Mikey, focusing on Titus's frustration with what he perceives as his boyfriend's incessant babbling on topics of little interest to him. Ever-helpful Kimmy suggests a listening or, rather, pseudolistening strategy which she employed in the bunker. Yet as his communication with and understanding of Mikey improves over the course of the episode, Titus realizes Kimmy's ruse won't be necessary.

**Central Concepts**: Listening, Gender
**Related Concepts**: Convergence, Relational Stages, Disclosure, Empathy
**Length and Location of Scene 1**: Approximately 1 minute (~ 0:03:13–0:3:56)
**Opening Line**: "Last night, Goatzilla flubbed his line again."
**Closing Line**: "When you try to put two five-foot rebars together . . ."
**Length and Location of Scene 2**: Approximately 2 minutes (~ 0:08:10–0:9:53)
**Opening Line**: "I met a really cute guy at a restaurant where I peed."
**Closing Line**: "Kimpanzee, you lived through a nightmare, but you learned so much cool stuff."
**Length and Location of Scene 3**: Approximately 1 minute (~ 0:14:02–0:15:10)
**Opening Line**: "My nonno, he insists on still having a garden."
**Closing Line**: "Eh."
**Length and Location of Scene 4**: Approximately 1 minute (~ 0:18:30–0:19:26)
**Opening Line**: "What are you doing, Titus? This looks terrible."
**Closing Line**: "And I once played a straight corpse on *America's Most Wanted*."
**Length and Location of Scene 5**: Approximately 1 minute (~ 0:23:08–0:24:25)
**Opening Line**: "Do go on."
**Closing Line**: "We just moved past this."
**Length and Location of Scene 6**: Approximately 1/2 minute (~ 0:23:08–0:24:25)
**Opening Line**: "And that's why I don't feel like I deserve my father's love."
**Closing Line**: "I have a tail. A little tail."

**Discussion Questions**
1. Contrast the listening style and responses that Titus employs with Mikey in the first scene compared to those he employs with Kimmy in the second scene.
2. Describe the linguistic convergence that occurs in scene #3 with Titus, Mikey, and his construction coworkers.
3. In Scene 4, while arranging flowers and speaking to Kimmy about his relationship with Mikey, Titus distinguishes between two activities, which is an important distinction in communication theory. What is this distinction? How does Titus also reveal empathy for Mikey here?
4. At which of Knapp's relational stages do Titus and Mikey appear to be in these scenes?
5. What does the final scene suggest about gender, communication, and self-disclosure?

## Season 3, Episode 6: "Kimmy Is a Feminist"

In this episode, Kimmy, who received a rowing scholarship to Columbia, decides to attend a party with her rowing teammates, who also consider themselves feminists. Kimmy finds their feminist banter compelling, "smart" talk on topics new to Kimmy such as gender-normative behavior, Simone de Beauvoir, and "seventh-wave" feminism. Impressed by their jargon, Kimmy is eager to learn more from her friends and model their behavior. A makeover for Kimmy that features make-up, high heels, and a tight dress (dressing up for herself they argue is a feminist statement) precedes the party. Yet after witnessing the immature, drunken antics that ensue later in the evening, Kimmy concludes they're not as intelligent or evolved as she initially thought.

**Central Concepts**: Gender, Feminism
**Related Concepts**: Language, Microaggression, Stereotypes
**Length and Location of Scene 1**: Approximately 2 minutes (~ 0:00:28–0:2:40)
**Opening Line**: "This party is a rejection of Valentine's Day because it's so regressive."
**Closing Line**: "Oh brother. Help me."
**Length and Location of Scene 2**: Approximately 1/2 minute (~ 0:04:02–0:4:38)
**Opening Line**: "I look like a hooker."
**Closing Line**: "I'm a feminist. I think we should get to vote."

### Discussion Questions
1. In the first scene, the earnest description of Austin as "so woke" is intended to be funny. But what does it more seriously mean to be woke in the context of communication? What criteria would this entail?
2. What is a microaggression? And what kind of microaggression do the feminists feel Austin committed? Why is gendered language of this sort potentially problematic? Identify other instances where more inclusive, gender-neutral language would be more appropriate.
3. Provide examples of other microaggressions in communication.
4. Describe the debates about "sexy feminism" and "heroic sex workers" satirized in the second scene. What role does clothing play in gendered communication for women and for men?
5. Does the satiric treatment of feminists in this episode give actual feminism a bad name? Are these harmful stereotypes? How do you define feminism? What makes men and even women reluctant to identify as feminists? How has the #MeToo phenoenon changed public perception of the feminist movement?

# SECTION III
# FULL-LENGTH FEATURE FILMS

Each of the film entries in this section provides information in the following categories:

*Film Data*: Year, Director, Length, and Rating
*Cast:* Principal roles in the film
*Communication Concepts:* Communication concepts that can be illustrated through the film (listed alphabetically)
*Viewing Information*: Introduction and viewing notes for the film, indicating audience
*Synopsis*: Summary of the film's plot and themes
*Discussion Questions*: Questions (and answers) linking the film to communication concepts

The discussion questions are the heart of this section. The questions posed are not the only ones that can or should be asked, nor are the answers given for the films the only "right" way to respond to the questions. In fact, you may argue with some of the analyses and interpretations. That's fine—any good discussion about movies should engender disagreement. The questions and answers are provided simply to offer you direction and data for analyzing the movies.

This book is designed as an ancillary for communication textbooks that focus on primarily on interpersonal and group communication concepts. Whenever possible, terms from these texts are used in the film entries, particularly in the discussion questions and their responses. The responses suggest some, but certainly not all, of the ways the discussion questions can be answered with concepts from the textbooks. It is likely that other communication issues beyond the ones identified can be found in the films. Thus, the entries should be seen as comprehensive but not exhaustive. If and when they stimulate new ideas, please share those ideas through letters, e-mail, papers, and articles.

# (500) DAYS OF SUMMER

| Film Data | |
|---|---|
| Year | 2009 |
| Director | Marc Webb |
| Length | 95 minutes |
| Rating | PG-13 |

| Main Cast | |
|---|---|
| **Character** | **Actor** |
| Tom Hansen | Joseph Gordon-Levitt |
| Summer Finn | Zooey Deschanel |

## Communication Concepts

Attachment Styles
Commitment
Nonverbal Miscommunication
Relational Development and Dialectics

## Viewing Information

In an ominous tone, a voice utters the opening line of the film: "This is not a love story." Indeed, it is not. Tom Hansen is a shy, hopeless romantic who writes greeting card lines for a living. Seemingly out of nowhere, Summer Finn walks into his life, and Tom is smitten at first sight. One problem, though: Summer does not believe in romance. Tom pursues Summer anyway, and although they do become involved romantically, Tom learns several painful lessons about unrequited love. Remember, this is not a love story.

## Synopsis

Tom Hansen thought he had found "the one." Like her seasonal namesake, Summer Finn blew into Tom's life unexpectedly, and he was a changed man—though perhaps not for the better. *(500) Days of Summer* opens with Tom severely depressed, mourning his break-up with Summer. In non-linear fashion, the rest of the film portrays Tom's reflections on their relationship leading up to, and after, their break-up. Along the way, we are treated to moments of misunderstood signals, ruminations on romance, and a conflict of commitment.

*Discussion Questions*
1. Identify Tom and Summer's stages of relational development, including their coming together and coming apart stages. How are differences in commitment demonstrated in these stages? How do the characters experience and manage the predictability versus novelty dialectic?
2. Use attachment styles theory to label Tom and Summer's perspectives on love and relationships, and identify examples of their attachment styles. Are their different attachment styles necessarily incompatible? Explain.
3. Locate moments when Tom has difficulty reading Summer's nonverbal cues. Does Tom have poor nonverbal decoding skills, or is Summer difficult to read? What are their content and relational level meanings?

# AMERICAN HUSTLE

| Film Data | |
| --- | --- |
| Year | 2013 |
| Director | David O. Russell |
| Length | 138 minutes |
| Rating | R |

| Main Cast | |
| --- | --- |
| **Character** | **Actor** |
| Irving Rosenfeld | Christian Bale |
| Richard "Richie" DiMaso | Bradley Cooper |
| Sydney Prosser | Amy Adams |
| Mayor Carmine Polito | Jeremy Renner |
| Rosalyn Rosenfeld | Jennifer Lawrence |

## Communication Concepts

Public/Private Self and Identity Management
Self-Concept/Looking-Glass Self/Self-Fulfilling Prophecy
Stereotypes/Prototypes/Scripts
Confirming/Disagreeing/Disconfirming Messages
Communication Climate

## Viewing Information

*American Hustle* is, in many ways, a period piece. From the hairstyles, to the wardrobes, to the soundtrack, director David O. Russell throws audiences back into the 1970s. Perhaps one of the most tantalizing aspects of the film is that there are five fully fledged, complex characters, each with neuroses, flaws, and endearing qualities. One could even argue that there are five main characters. *American Hustle* was released to critical acclaim, and for good reason. The film is rated R for sexual material, some violence, profanity, and scenes containing substance abuse—all depicted artfully, so as to capture the essence of a time period.

*Synopsis*

Loosely based on the FBI ABSCAM operation that took place as the 1970s transitioned into the 1980s, *American Hustle* centers on con artists Irving Rosenfeld and Sydney Prosser who are forced by FBI agent Richie DiMaso to engineer an intricate sting operation in an attempt to expose corrupt politicians. Richie's prime target becomes Camden, New Jersey's Mayor Carmine Polito. As Irving is pulled more and more deeply into a scam he knows is doomed to fail, he must not only negotiate the two women in his life—his current mistress and partner Sydney, and his unpredictable wife Rosalyn—but save himself and those around him from almost assured prosecution.

*Discussion Questions*
1. The five main characters (Irving, Richie, Sydney, Mayor Carmine, and Rosalyn) are wildly different individuals, each with strong personalities. What stereotype does each character fulfill? What scripts do the characters follow? Choose two of the five main characters and analyze their self-concept. Use the terms *looking-glass self* and *self-fulfilling prophecy* in your analysis.
2. Discuss self-concept in relation to *American Hustle*'s two leading female characters, Sydney Prosser (Amy Adams) and Rosalyn Rosenfeld (Jennifer Lawrence). Explain how their self-conceptions are similar and/or different.
3. *American Hustle* contains many volatile relationships. How is the idea of confirming/disagreeing/disconfirming messages, in the context of a relationship, present in the film? Which relationships best display this concept?

# ARGO

## Film Data

| Year | 2012 |
|---|---|
| Director | Ben Affleck |
| Length | 120 minutes |
| Rating | R |

## Main Cast

| Character | Actor |
|---|---|
| Tony Mendez | Ben Affleck |
| Jack O'Donnell | Bryan Cranston |
| Lester Siegel | Alan Arkin |
| John Chambers | John Goodman |
| Bob Anders | Tate Donovan |
| Joe Stafford | Scoot McNairy |
| Kathy Stafford | Kerry Bishé |
| Lee Schatz | Rory Cochrane |
| Cora Lijek | Clea DuVall |
| Mark Lijek | Christopher Denham |

## Communication Concepts

Group Cohesiveness
Group Decision-Making
Group Roles
Leadership
Problem-Solving in Groups

## Viewing Information

Although based on actual events that occurred early in the Iran hostage crisis (1979-1981), *Argo* is a dramatization and fictionalized account of one particular group's experience. A suspense-thriller, the film stars and is directed by Ben Affleck. His character, Tony Mendez, hatches a plan to rescue six American diplomats who managed to avoid being taken hostage but are also trapped in Iran. In order to carry out his plan to bring them home, Mendez seeks help from two major Hollywood players: special effects wizard John Chambers (John Goodman) and film producer Lester Siegel (Alan Arkin). Together, they intend to rescue the six diplomats with an implausible idea: pretend they are a Canadian film crew on location in Iran and fly them out on a commercial airliner. The film won the Oscar for Best Picture in 2013.

## Synopsis

The year is 1979, and the American embassy in Iran has just been overrun by a large group of radical militants. These militants take 52 Americans hostage, but the U.S. State Department learns that six American diplomats managed to escape and that they are currently under the protection of the Canadian Ambassador to Iran. Tony Mendez is a CIA operative known for his expertise in "exfiltration"—getting American citizens out of a foreign occupied country. When the U.S. State Department consults Mendez on how to exfiltrate the six American diplomats, he offers an unusual solution: disguise the six diplomats as a Canadian film crew on location and fly them out on a commercial airliner. As implausible as the idea seems, Mendez receives the go-ahead from the U.S. government. Now he just has to convince the six diplomats to go along with his plan and carry out the mission before the Iranian government discovers their true identities.

## Discussion Questions
1. Identify different stages of problem solving that occur during cabinet meetings with U.S. government officials. What specific steps do these groups take to solve problems? How does power influence this process?
2. Analyze the group communication among the six American diplomats, and examine their decision to follow Tony Mendez's plan. How does this group make decisions? Which group roles are demonstrated? How does group cohesiveness influence their decisions?
3. Consider Tony Mendez as a group leader. What traits does he possess that are typical of leaders? How would you describe his leadership style? How does Mendez adapt his style to match that of his followers (the six diplomats)?

# THE AVENGERS

| Film Data | |
|---|---|
| Year | 2012 |
| Director | Joss Whedon |
| Length | 143 minutes |
| Rating | PG-13 |

| Main Cast | |
|---|---|
| Character | Actor |
| Tony Stark/Iron Man | Robert Downey Jr. |
| Steve Rogers/Captain America | Chris Evans |
| Bruce Banner/the Hulk | Mark Ruffalo |
| Thor | Chris Hemsworth |
| Natasha Romanoff/Black Widow | Scarlett Johansson |
| Clint Barton/Hawkeye | Jeremy Renner |
| Loki | Tom Hiddleston |
| Agent Phil Coulson | Clark Gregg |
| Director Nick Fury | Samuel L. Jackson |

## Communication Concepts

Small-Group and Team Communication
Group Stages of Development
Leadership and Power

## Viewing Information

The sixth episode in the Marvel cinematic franchise, *The Avengers* became the high-grossing movie of 2012 and the highest-grossing superhero film to date. It owes its success to stunning visual effects but also to a compelling story that succeeds in humanizing its superheroes—humanity revealed largely in group interaction and dialogue. Through their interpersonal communication, the Avengers manifest strengths and vulnerabilities readily apparent to viewers, traits that are in some ways unique and in some ways universal. When a crisis situation of epic proportions requires them to act as a team, evidently even superheroes encounter many of the same group issues we might at our more pedestrian workplace or sports facility. And when this loose collection of individuals eventually unites as the Avengers, they experience the same enhanced performance toward a goal, the ideal for which any team strives.

## *Synopsis*

Nick Fury, the director of S.H.I.E.L.D., recruits a dream team of superheroes to confront a recent threat posed by Thor's evil brother, Loki, who, having failed in his quest to reign as king of Asgard, seeks not only possession of a mystical energy cube known as the Tessaract, but also world domination of Earth. In league with an alien army of Chitauri, Loki proceeds in his characteristically megalomaniacal manner to wreak havoc. Fury's response team is composed of Steve Rogers (a.k.a. Captain America), Tony Stark (a.k.a. Iron Man), Natasha Romanoff (a.k.a. Black Widow), Bruce Banner (a.k.a. Hulk), Thor (a.k.a. Prince of Asgard and Loki's brother), and Clinton Barton (a.k.a. Hawkeye). This union of formidable individuals must resolve conflict within the group before evolving into the high-functioning team we know as The Avengers. As members see past their differences, recognize each other's strengths, and assume certain roles within the developing team, commitment to their mission and group grows, producing a superhero squad capable of saving the world from the most destructive of forces.

## *Discussion Questions*
1.  Who exhibits leadership in this film, and how would you characterize the leadership style of each of these characters?
2.  Even those who have not assumed a decisive leadership role can still wield power in a group. Describe the different types of power, as defined in communication theory, exercised by the other members of the Avengers team.
3.  Describe the Avengers' stages of development using Bruce Tuckman's theoretical framework of forming, storming, norming, and performing. What role does group cohesiveness play in their movement from a group to a team?

# THE BIG SICK

## Film Data

| | |
|---|---|
| Year | 2017 |
| Director | Michael Showalter |
| Length | 120 minutes |
| Rating | R |

## Main Cast

| Character | Actor |
|---|---|
| Kumail | Kumail Nanjiani |
| Emily | Zoe Kazan |
| Beth | Holly Hunter |
| Terry | Ray Romero |
| Azmat | Anupam Kher |
| Sharmeen | Zenobia Shroff |
| Naveed | Adeel Akhtar |
| CJ | Bo Burnham |
| Mary | Aidy Bryant |
| Chris | Kurt Braunohler |
| Khadija | Vella Lovell |
| Sumera | Shunori Ramanathan |
| Nurse Judy | Myra Lucretia Taylor |
| Bob Dalavan | Jeremy Shamos |
| Andy Dodd | David Alan Grier |
| Sam Highsmith | Ed Herbstman |

## Communication Concepts

Honesty/Deception/Lies
Relational Stages
Communication Climate
Communication Competence

*Viewing Information*

Based on the early relationship of longtime spouses Kumail Nanjiani and Emily V. Gordon, *The Big Sick* is a semi-autobiographical story that features the interpersonal challenges faced by couples and families, and couples (or potential couples) within families. Despite a life-threatening illness that renders Emily unable to communicate with Kumail for considerable screen time, their early relational stages will resonate with millennial viewers who, recognizing temperamental affinities that should ideally eclipse cultural discrepencies, end up rooting for their future together. The relationship Kumail subsequently develops with Emily's parents introduces him to a different family dynamic, an open and transparent communication climate that contrasts with the style of his loving but traditional Pakistani family. Acclaimed by critics and audiences alike, *The Big Sick* is a feel-good story that manages to find humor in even the intensive care unit while providing more serious lessons about the kind of communication families and couples require for relational success. The film is rated R for language including some sexual references.

*Synopsis*

*The Big Sick* follows the rom-com formula of boy meets girl, boy loses girl, boy recovers girl. Less formulaic, however, is the cause of the predictable rupture, which takes the form of a culture clash between boy and girl. Kumail, a Pakistani American and stand-up comedian, meets Emily, a white psychology graduate student from North Carolina, at a comedy club in Chicago. Love-at-first-sight develops into a serious courtship that comes to a crashing halt when, after several months together, Emily discovers Kumail's secret: if he doesn't fulfill his traditional Pakistani parents' wish for an arranged Muslim marriage to a Pakistani woman, they will disown him. The big bust-up then becomes the big sick after Emily succumbs to a mysterious, life-threatening illness requiring a medically induced coma, a strange situation in which Kumail meets and develops an unexpected bond with Emily's parents. Torn between his love for his family and his recognition of his love for Emily, Kumail confronts a number of life-changing decisions. While the plot sounds like the stuff of fiction, it is based on true-life events in the relationship of Kumail Nanjiani, who plays himself, and his wife, Emily V. Gordon, who co-wrote the script with him.

*Discussion Questions*
1. Honesty, or lack thereof, is a unifying theme in The Big Sick. Describe the various kinds of untruths and deceptions dramatized in the film. Consider their ethical implications and consequences. What role does honesty play here in communication competence?
2. Compare the climate and pattern of communication in Emily's family with the dynamics in Kumail's. Consider their specific orientation on the dimensions of conversation and conformity. How does Geert Hofstede's intercultural communication theory help explain stylistic differences?
3. Describe Kumail and Emily's relationship using Knapp's developmental model of relational stages.

# THE BREAKFAST CLUB

| Film Data | |
|---|---|
| Year | 1985 |
| Director | John Hughes |
| Length | 92 minutes |
| Rating | R |

| Main Cast | |
|---|---|
| **Character** | **Actor** |
| Andrew Clark | Emilio Estevez |
| Richard Vernon | Paul Gleason |
| Brian Johnson | Anthony Michael Hall |
| John Bender | Judd Nelson |
| Claire Standish | Claire Standish |
| Allison Reynolds | Ally Sheedy |

## Communication Concepts

Critical Thinking
Group Cohesiveness
Group Development
Perception
Power
Roles
Self-Disclosure
Status

## Viewing Information

The movie clearly subscribes to an "ideology of intimacy." The moral of the story appears to be that openness and honesty—even with complete strangers—will make a person happy, healthy, and wise. Something to think about as you watch the film is "Do you think the members of the Breakfast Club will remain friends?" While those who love happy endings may answer yes, many realistically acknowledge that peer pressure from the members' cliques will keep them from interacting on Monday. If this is true, then the five teenagers in the movie have handed intimate, personal, and private information to people who may be their social enemies (or at least competitors) at school. In a worst-case scenario, their self-disclosures could become inter-clique arsenal in the weeks that follow. The pros and cons of self-disclosure are an integral issue in *The Breakfast Club*.

## Synopsis

*The Breakfast Club* takes place at an Illinois high school, where five dissimilar students are sentenced to spend a Saturday detention session together. In attendance is a "princess" (Ringwald), an "athlete" (Estevez), a "brain" (Hall), a "criminal" (Nelson), and a "basket case" (Sheedy). These titles identify the roles the students play during the school week. Because of stereotypes and status levels associated with each role, the students want nothing to do with each other at the outset of the session. However, when confronted by the authoritarian detention teacher (Gleason) and by eight hours of time to kill, the students begin to interact. Through self-disclosure they learn that they are more similar than different. Each wrestles with self-acceptance; each longs for parental approval; each fights against peer pressure. They break through the role barriers and gain greater understanding and acceptance of each other and of themselves. They ultimately develop a group identity and dub themselves "The Breakfast Club."

## Discussion Questions
1. How do the characters deviate from their normal roles during the detention session?
2. What is the status of each character prior to the detention session? How does this change during their detention session?
3. What power resources and discussion roles are exhibited in the movie?
4. Discuss the group's developmental stages.
5. What factors contribute to the group's cohesiveness?
6. Discuss the role that perception and stereotyping play in this movie.

# EASY A

| Film Data | |
|---|---|
| Year | 2010 |
| Director | Will Gluck |
| Length | 25 minutes |
| Rating | PG-13 |

| Main Cast | |
|---|---|
| Character | Actor |
| Olive Penderghast | Emma Stone |
| Marianne | Amanda Bynes |
| Rhiannon | Alyson Michalka |
| Mr. Griffith | Thomas Haden Church |
| Mrs. Griffith | Lisa Kudrow |
| Rosemary Penderghast | Patricia Clarkson |
| Dill Penderghast | Stanley Tucci |

## Communication Concepts

Computer-Mediated Communication
Face Maintenance
Identity Management

## Viewing Information

Set and filmed on location in idyllic Ojai, California, *Easy A* stars Emma Stone is Olive Penderghast: a once invisible high school student, now with a bad reputation. Intentionally written to resemble a John Hughes movie from the 1980s (*Ferris Bueller's Day Off, Pretty in Pink, Sixteen Candles*), this comedy explores how high school rumors get started, how they spread, and their strong influence on perceptions. The film also has a star-studded ensemble cast, including Stanley Tucci and Patricia Clarkson as Olive's parents, Thomas Haden Church as her favorite teacher, and Lisa Kudrow as the school guidance counselor.

*Synopsis*

*Easy A* recounts the tale of Olive Penderghast, a clean-cut high school girl whose reputation quickly takes a turn for the worse. When Olive lies to her best friend about losing her virginity, the school's rumor mill takes over. Olive's image is transformed seemingly overnight, and she starts to notice that her life resembles that of Hester Prynne, Nathaniel Hawthorne's adulteress in *The Scarlet Letter*. Recognizing that she can capitalize both financially and socially on her new status, Olive embraces the role. However, she soon realizes that pretending to be an overly sexualized teenager is a lot more fun than actually being one. Having lost her best friend and on the verge of being expelled, can Olive squash these rumors and repair her lost identity?

*Discussion Questions*
1. Identify examples of Olive's identity management. How does Olive's perceived self compare to her presenting self, and how do these two selves change during the course of the film?
2. How do the characters engage in facework? Which characters are more concerned about their public face? Which characters are willing to give face to others?
3. *Easy A* illustrates how quickly a rumor can travel. Thinking about rumors specifically and information in general, how has technology changed the way information flows among people? How does the channel (e.g., texting) affect both the credibility of the source and the information itself?

# THE GREAT DEBATERS

| Film Data | |
|---|---|
| Year | 2007 |
| Director | Denzel Washington |
| Length | 126 minutes |
| Rating | PG-13 |

| Main Cast | |
|---|---|
| Character | Actor |
| Melvin B. Tolson | Denzel Washington |
| Henry Lowe | Nate Parker |
| Samantha Booke | Jurnee Smollett |
| James Farmer Jr | Denzel Whitaker |
| Dr. James Farmer Sr | Forest Whitaker |
| Hamilton Burgess | Jermaine Williams |
| Sheriff Dozier | John Heard |

## Communication Concepts

Leadership
Persuasive Appeals (Ethos, Pathos, Logos)
Power in Groups
Small-Group Cohesiveness
Social Judgment Theory

## Viewing Information

Based on the true story of the 1935 Wiley College Debate Team, this film is a dramatic account of confronting intolerance through speech. With eloquent oratory, the film illustrates well how persuasion can be used to change minds, and history. Students should recognize Denzel Washington and Forest Whitaker in their respective roles as debate coach and professor. However, it is the cast of young actors portraying the debate team who deserves consideration.

*Synopsis*

*The Great Debaters* is a moving, inspirational story about how the power of speech can overcome prejudice. The film is set in southern Texas in the 1930s, a time and place of racial intolerance, where Jim Crow laws were still on the books and lynchings were a common spectacle. At small, historically-black Wiley College, students on the debate team not only challenge each other, they confront the prevailing social ideologies head-on. With the help of their charismatic and eloquent coach, real-life poet Melvin B. Tolson, the Wiley College Debate Team gains national recognition as one of the first black colleges to debate white students. Their prominence culminates with a nationally broadcast debate with Harvard University. In the end the debaters gain more than a simple victory, they gain respect for themselves and their race.

*Discussion Questions*
1. Identify examples of social judgment theory, including latitudes of acceptance, rejection, and noncommitment. How does ego-involvement influence the persuasive process?
2. How do the debaters utilize appeals to ethos, pathos, and logos in their arguments? Which type of appeal do you find most persuasive? Why?
3. Explain the factors or reasons why the Wiley College Debaters become a cohesive group.
4. Identify examples of power used by the characters. Which types of power are effective? Which types are appropriate?

# HELLO, MY NAME IS DORIS

## Film Data

| | |
|---|---|
| Year | 2015 |
| Director | Michael Showalter |
| Length | 95 minutes |
| Rating | R |

## Main Cast

| Character | Actor |
|---|---|
| Doris | Sally Field |
| John | Max Greenfield |
| Roz | Tyne Daly |
| Vivian | Isabelle Acres |
| Todd | Stephen Root |
| Willy Williams | Peter Gallagher |
| Dr. Edwards | Elizabeth Reaser |

## Communication Concepts

Prejudice
Identity Management
Self-Concept/Presenting Self/Perceived Self
Reflected Appraisal
Self-Fulfilling Prophecy
Convergence

## Viewing Information

In another critically acclaimed performance, Sally Field shines in this indie flick as a lonely sixty-something office drone who earnestly seeks the romance that she sacrificed in her youth to care for her mother. Clichés of both the old and the young abound. Doris is a hoarder and a cat lady; her much younger new cohort, pretentious hipsters. Both sets of stereotypes alternately amuse and dismay, but Doris remains throughout a sympathetic protagonist whose journey of self-discovery transcends the stereotypical while raising a number of important questions about second acts and May–December relationships.

*Synopsis*

Following the death of her mother, Doris sets out to reinvent herself in the hope of attracting the romantic attentions of a handsome new coworker who instantly became the object of her latent desire. Although her best friend fears she is making a fool of herself by desperately pursuing a hopelessly younger man, the relationship Doris succeeds in developing with John is not entirely without substance or merit. While the romantic path she charts for herself does not end where she envisioned, Doris learns from her new interpersonal relationships (some of these lessons are inevitably painful), grows over the course of the film, and ultimately redefines her identify and life in ways that leave the audience hopeful for her future.

*Discussion Questions*
1. Which societal prejudice does this film primarily explore?
2. Describe how Doris's identity management intensifies after meeting John. In what sense are her efforts at reinventing herself after her mother's death a self-fulfilling prophecy? How would you describe her evolving self-concept, particularly the relationship between her presenting self and her perceived self?
3. What role does convergence through verbal and nonverbal communication play in Doris's self-transformation? How does reflected appraisal affect her self-concept?

# HIDDEN FIGURES

| Film Data | |
|---|---|
| Year | 2016 |
| Director | Theodore Melfi |
| Length | 127 minutes |
| Rating | PG |

| Main Cast | |
|---|---|
| **Character** | **Actor** |
| Katherine G. Johnson | Taraji P. Henson |
| Dorothy Vaughn | Octavia Spencer |
| Mary Jackson | Janelle Monáe |
| Al Harrison | Kevin Costner |
| Vivian Mitchell | Kirsten Dunst |
| Paul Stafford | Jim Parsons |
| Colonel Jim Johnson | Mahershala Ali |
| Levi Jackson | Aldis Hodge |
| John Glenn | Glen Powell |
| Ruth | Kimberly Quinn |
| Karl Zielinski | Olek Krupa |

## Communication Concepts

Intersectionality
Standpoint Theory
Prejudice
Stereotypes
Leadership

*Viewing Information*

*Hidden Figures* shines a light on the largely hidden stories of three black mathematicians, members of different teams at the Langley Research Center whose varied contributions were critical to the success of the American space race. Although many of the scenes and situations were embellished for dramatic effect, these women were actual historic figures, their inspirational life stories a welcome challenge to the professional stereotypes that still plague STEM (science, technology, engineering, and math) fields. A critical and box-office success, the film depicts the interpersonal communication that occurred behind the scientific scenes and ultimately permitted their rise to unprecedented heights, accomplishments all the more singular for the prejudices these women confronted at the intersection of race and gender. *Hidden Figures* also illustrates key concepts and subjects in organizational communication, notably leadership. This film is rated PG for thematic elements and some language. The times are based on streaming the movie on HBO.

*Synopsis*

Project Mercury, the American space program established to achieve the first manned orbital flight, forms the big-picture historic backdrop of *Hidden Figures*. But the principal dramatic focus is on the significant trails blazed in the 1960s by three black women at the Langley Research Center in Hampton, Virginia. Katherine Johnson, Dorothy Vaughn, and Mary Jackson were "computers" in the fields of science, technology, engineering, and mathematics long before STEM existed as an acronym. These colleagues and friends set precedents in their respective fields while confronting the racial biases of the era in a state clinging to segregation, as well as the gendered expectations held by men and women. Ultimately, there are no villains in *Hidden Figures* as certain key NASA personnel, looking beyond race and gender, were able to recognize and utilize their exceptional talents. *Hidden Figures* is a story of figures revealed, indomitable spirits who overcame a number of formidable obstacles in their stellar careers.

*Discussion Questions*
1. Describe the systemic prejudice illustrated in this story. Which groups are the principal targets of discrimination? How does standpoint theory help explain the interpersonal communication and dynamics that this power disparity produces?
2. Define intersectionality, and explain its role in Hidden Figures. Describe how membership in multiple groups shapes identity for the three protagonists. How does the film's foregrounding of intersectionality help combat stereotyping?
3. Who are the nominal team leaders at Langley, and how would you characterize the leadership and managerial styles of these individuals?

# A HOLOGRAM FOR THE KING

| Film Data | |
|---|---|
| Year | 2016 |
| Director | Tom Tykwer |
| Length | 98 minutes |
| Rating | R |

| Main Cast | |
|---|---|
| Character | Actor |
| Alan | Tom Hanks |
| Yousef | Alexander Black |
| Zahra | Sarita Choudhoury |
| Hanne | Sidse Babett Knudsen |
| Kit | Tracey Fairaway |

## Communication Concepts

Culture Shock
Collectivism/Individualism
Power Distance
Uncertainty Avoidance
Team Leadership and Communication
Intercultural Competence

## Viewing Information

Despite what was generally acknowledged as a fine performance by Tom Hanks, this film received mixed to average reviews and underperformed at the box office. The movie not being a big hit for Hanks, however, does not diminish the value of a story that illustrates a number of complexities of intercultural communication. And audiences will still root for Alan as he overcomes his initial intercultural ineptitude, a source of drama and comedy, and develops meaningful relationships that bode well for his personal and professional future.

## Synopsis

Following a bitter divorce and the loss of his home, business sales rep Alan Clay (Tom Hanks) experiences a mid-life crisis that plays out in the desert, where he becomes an Everyman's Alan of Arabia. Hoping to turn his life around by brokering a lucrative international deal, he has persuaded his overbearing boss that he can sell a holographic teleconferencing system to the Saudi king. Much is riding on the success of this venture, including his daughter's college education and his tenuous position within the Relyand organization. The affable if depressed Alan experiences culture shock on his arrival in the Kingdom of Saudi Arabia, having done little apparently to prepare himself or his team for what to expect as strangers in a strange land. Fortunately, he befriends an irreverent cabbie and a beautiful doctor who help him navigate the physical and cultural terrain of the desert. In an unexpected turn of events, Alan manages to develop significant interpersonal and intercultural relationships that result in an extended sojourn in Saudi Arabia.

## Discussion Questions

1. Describe the collectivist nature of Saudi Arabia dramatized in the film? What other cultural factors besides collectivism influence Saudi behavior and communication? Which of Geert Hofstede's dimensions most prominently shape Saudi culture?
2. Compare Alan's interaction and leadership with his team to the organizational communication apparent among Saudis.
3. How would you rate Alan's intercultural competence? What errors does he make, and what might he have done to improve his intercultural communication skills?

# THE KIDS ARE ALL RIGHT

### Film Data

| | |
|---|---|
| Year | 2010 |
| Director | Lisa Cholodenko |
| Length | 105 minutes |
| Rating | R |

### Main Cast

| Character | Actor |
|---|---|
| Nic | Annette Bening |
| Jules | Julianne Moore |
| Joni | Mia Wasikowska |
| Laser | Josh Hutcherson |
| Paul | Mark Ruffalo |

### Communication Concepts

Communication Conflict
Content and Relational Messages
Metacommunication
Relational Control

### Viewing Information

Have you ever felt that your family is the only one with parents who constantly nag you, or who never seem to understand where you're coming from? Well, think again. In the film *The Kids Are All Right*, Director Lisa Cholodenko presents the typical American family. Yes, the parents happen to be two gay women (played by Julianne Moore and Annette Bening) who each gave birth to a child (played by Josh Hutcherson and Mia Wasikowska, respectively) from the same sperm donor, but push those details aside. Otherwise, you might miss the film's relevant and nuanced examples of family communication. And you might just realize that your own annoying parents actually care an awful lot about you.

*Synopsis*

Nic and Jules are living the American family script: two successful, upper-middle class parents raising their two children in Southern California. Joni, the older child, is about to head off to college, and her brother Laser is quickly becoming a young man. By the way, Nic and Jules are two gay women who gave birth to their children with the same sperm donor. When Laser pressures Joni to make contact with Paul, the donor, their entire family system is thrown off balance. Through conflicts brought on by Paul's influence and misunderstood intentions, Nic and Jules struggle to redefine their changing relationship and let go of their independence-craving children.

*Discussion Questions*
1. Identify examples of metacommunication that Nic and Jules use in their relationship. Are these metamessages effective in solving their conflicts? Please explain.
2. Locate examples of content and relational messages. When are there misunderstandings between what was said and how it was said? What effect do these misunderstandings have on the relationships among the characters?
3. Take a close look at all four family members, and analyze their different combinations of relational control. Which relationships are complementary? Which are symmetrical? Provide examples.

# *LARS AND THE REAL GIRL*

### Film Data

| Film Data | |
|---|---|
| Year | 2007 |
| Director | Craig Gillespie |
| Length | 106 minutes |
| Rating | PG-13 |

### Main Cast

| Main Cast | |
|---|---|
| Character | Actor |
| Lars | Ryan Gosling |
| Karin | Emily Mortimer |
| Gus | Paul Schneider |
| Dr. Dagmar | Patricia Clarkson |
| Margo | Kelli Garner |

## Communication Concepts

Coordinated Management of Meaning Theory
Relational Dialectics
Relationship Stages
Symbolic Interactionism Theory

## Viewing Information

If you only read the DVD jacket of *Lars and the Real Girl*, you might conclude that the plot is hard to believe. On the contrary, this critically acclaimed film provides touching moments of community support and interpersonal understanding. Gosling gives a memorable performance as Lars, a delusional man searching for intimacy.

## Synopsis

Lars Lindstrom is a shy, sweet man who lives by himself in his brother's garage. When Lars brings his new girlfriend (Bianca) home to meet his brother (Gus) and sister-in-law (Karin), they are thrilled—until they learn that she is an anatomically correct mannequin. At the urging of their family doctor, Gus and Karin go along with Lars's delusion. Eventually, the whole town treats Lars and Bianca as if their relationship is real. The film shows how an entire community can come together to support one individual, and how communication works to create our reality.

*Discussion Questions*
1. Do Lars and Bianca have a "real" interpersonal relationship?
2. Apply Knapp's stages of development and decline to the relationship between Lars and Bianca.
3. Using symbolic interactionism theory (meaning, language, and thought), describe how the characters co-construct their reality through communication. How does the community of townspeople, the generalized other, contribute to the film's narrative?
4. Apply Coordinated Management of Meaning (CMM) theory to the film by explaining the regulative and constitutive rules the characters follow, including both coordinated and uncoordinated meanings.

# MONEYBALL

### Film Data

| | |
|---|---|
| Year | 2011 |
| Director | Bennett Miller |
| Length | 133 minutes |
| Rating | PG-13 |

### Main Cast

| Character | Actor |
|---|---|
| Billy Beane | Brad Pitt |
| Peter Brand | Jonah Hill |
| Art Howe | Philip Seymour Hoffman |
| Grady Fuson | Ken Medlock |
| David Justice | Stephen Bishop |

### Communication Concepts

Leadership
Power in Groups
Problem Solving in Groups

### Viewing Information

Brad Pitt is Billy Beane, the cunning yet charming General Manager of the Oakland Athletics Major League Baseball team. Based on Michael Lewis's book by the same name, *Moneyball* is set during the team's 2002 baseball season. The film chronicles their remarkable success on the field, and the secret formula that built the team. Sprinkled with clips of actual baseball games and cast with actors playing real baseball players, *Moneyball* is especially appealing for the sports enthusiast. Rounding out the cast, Peter Brand (Jonah Hill) is Beane's statistical genius, and Art Howe (Philip Seymour Hoffman) is the Athletics player Manager.

*Synopsis*

It is the 2001 Major League Baseball playoffs, and the cash-strapped Oakland Athletics have just lost to the money-rich New York Yankees. General Manager of the Athletics, Billy Beane (Brad Pitt), is beside himself with frustration and borderline anger. When it's time to assemble the 2002 team, and he learns that his star players are leaving for higher-paying contracts, Beane feels lost. On a scouting trip Beane meets Peter Brand (Jonah Hill), a recent Yale graduate with an economics degree and an apparent savant with regard to baseball statistics. Brand eventually convinces Beane to adopt his formula for evaluating players. What follows is a remarkable season by a most improbable team of misfits and castoffs who comprise the 2002 Oakland Athletics.

*Discussion Questions*
1. Identify examples of group problem solving, particularly during Beane's meetings with his scouts. What specific steps does the group take to make decisions? Which group roles are demonstrated?
2. Consider Billy Beane as a leader. What traits does he possess that are typical of leaders? How would you describe his leadership style? In what ways does his style change throughout the film?
3. How does Billy Beane demonstrate power in the film? What about his scouts and coaches? How does this use of power create conflict?

# OFFICE SPACE

### Film Data

| Year | 1999 |
|---|---|
| Director | Mike Judge |
| Length | 88 minutes |
| Rating | R |

### Main Cast

| Character | Actor |
|---|---|
| Peter Gibbons | Ron Livingston |
| Joanna | Jennifer Aniston |
| Milton Waddams | Stephen Root |
| Samir Nagheenanajar | Ajay Naidu |
| Michael Bolton | David Herman |
| Bill Lumbergh | Gary Cole |

### Communication Concepts

Classical Theory/Theory X
Communication Climate
Conflict
Honesty/Lying
Language
Self-Concept/Identity Management

### Viewing Information

The back cover of the *Office Space* video proudly announces that the film is by Mike Judge, creator of *Beavis and Butt-head*, which should serve as a warning that the movie has some crude content and language (as well as two brief sexual scenes). While this is a very humorous film, it touches on some serious issues that can be explored. (For example, see "Investigating the Relationship Between Superior–Subordinate Relationship Quality and Employee Dissent" by J. W. Kassing in *Communication Research Reports* [2000], Vol. 17, pp. 58–69).

One of the unstated morals of *Office Space* is that Peter's life becomes better when he stops closely managing his identity and begins doing and saying whatever he wants. While this makes for an entertaining movie (and is the premise for other entertaining films such as *Liar Liar*), the outcomes of Peter's decisions can and should be a point of discussion for communication students. Would Peter actually be promoted to management if he ignored his boss, came to work whenever he wanted, dressed in shorts, destroyed company property, and admitted his lack of motivation to outside consultants? Probably only in Hollywood, which makes this a good case study for debating the pros and cons of identity management, honesty, and rhetorical sensitivity in the workplace.

## Synopsis

Peter Gibbons (Livingston) and his colleagues Samir (Naidu) and Michael (Herman) are computer specialists who are fed up with their mundane jobs. They work at Initech Corporation, an impersonal organization with a Classical Theory/Theory X approach to management. Their boss, Lumbergh (Cole), has a condescending attitude and creates a defensive communication climate with all employees, including Milton (Root), the emotionally challenged mailroom clerk who keeps threatening to "burn the building." In a hypotherapy session, Peter loses his inhibitions and starts speaking his mind around the office. His "straight shooting" earns him a promotion while others are downsized out of the company. Peter and his colleagues carry out a high-tech embezzling scheme to get revenge on Initech. Peter's new girlfriend, Joanna (Aniston), is also fed up with her waitress job and her manager; however, she helps Peter realize that embezzling is an unethical way to handle his frustration with Initech. Ultimately, Peter and his friends move on to new horizons and Initech (quite literally) goes up in flames.

## Discussion Questions
1. Describe how the Initech Corporation illustrates Classical Theory and Theory X approaches to organizational communication.
2. Describe the communication climate in manager–employee interactions in the movie.
3. What styles of conflict management are used by the managers and employees in the movie?
4. Describe the changes Peter experiences in his identity management.

# OUTSOURCED

| Film Data | |
|---|---|
| Year | 2006 |
| Director | John Jeffcoat |
| Length | 103 minutes |
| Rating | PG-13 |

| Main Cast | |
|---|---|
| **Character** | **Actor** |
| Todd Anderson | Josh Hamilton |
| Asha | Ayesha Dharker |
| Puro | Asif Basra |
| Dave | Matt Smith |

## Communication Concepts

Adapting to Diversity
Culture Shock
Individualism and Collectivism
Organizational Culture
Proxemics

## Viewing Information

A light-hearted comedy with a likable cast, *Outsourced* provides examples of contemporary business practices in the same way *Office Space* put the spotlight on the cubicle culture. Part cross-cultural sojourn and part international business, the film attempts to capture what happens when your job, and everyone who works for you, is outsourced to India. Hamilton portrays the business everyman, Dharker is his opinionated love interest, and Basra is Todd's charming and energetic replacement.

## Synopsis

So far, the life of Todd Anderson has been predictable and uneventful. He manages a customer service call center in Seattle, for a company selling novelty products. His world is turned upside down when his job, and everyone under him, is outsourced to India. If being fired weren't bad enough, Todd's boss strong-arms him into going to India to train his replacement. In India Todd is overwhelmed by the cultural differences, both in and out of the new call center. He eventually finds a way to train his new staff and increase their productivity, but not before Todd learns something about himself.

## Discussion Questions

1. Identify examples of Todd's culture shock, including his loss of personal space. Also, apply Edward Hall's distances in your explanation.
2. Recognize examples of Todd's individualism and the host culture's collectivism.
3. Provide examples that illustrate Todd's process of adapting to cultural diversity (i.e., resistance, tolerance, understanding, respect, and participation).
4. Analyze the organizational culture of the call center when Todd first arrives compared to the end of the film, including their rituals and customs. How was Todd able to motivate the employees and change their organizational culture?

# SILVER LININGS PLAYBOOK

| Film Data | |
|---|---|
| Year | 2012 |
| Director | David O. Russell |
| Length | 124 minutes |
| Rating | R |

| Main Cast | |
|---|---|
| **Character** | **Actor** |
| Pat Solitano Jr. | Bradley Cooper |
| Tiffany | Jennifer Lawrence |
| Pat Solitano Sr. | Robert De Niro |
| Dolores Solitano | Jacki Weaver |
| Jake Solitano | Shea Whigham |
| Ronnie | John Ortiz |

## Communication Concepts

Communication Climate
Communication Competence
Conflict
Family Communication

## Viewing Information

*Silver Linings Playbook* is a romantic comedy unlike most other films of the genre. Indeed, when one of the protagonists (Pat Jr., played by Bradley Cooper) suffers from bipolar disorder, and the other (Tiffany, played by Jennifer Lawrence) takes medication for severe depression, their interpersonal communication is sure to be unique. And let's not forget that Pat's father (Robert De Niro) is a highly superstitious gambler whose behavior borders on obsessive-compulsive disorder. When his mother (Dolores, played by Jacki Weaver) brings Pat home following a stay in a mental health facility, the family's interaction patterns are combustible. Surprisingly, Tiffany might be the antidote this family needs to help cure their dysfunctional communication.

## Synopsis

Pat always knew in the back of his mind that he had undiagnosed mental health problems. Unfortunately for him, he had to lose his job, his marriage, and his freedom before he sought treatment for his bipolar disorder. When he is released from a mental health facility into his mother's custody, Pat swears that he wants to get his life back on track. Despite his estranged wife's restraining order against him, Pat intends to prove to her that he is a different, better person, beginning with a letter he intends to send her. In order to do this, however, Pat has to make a bargain with Tiffany, a mysterious friend of his wife's who has some mental issues of her own. Tiffany is a dancer, and she needs Pat to be her partner for an upcoming dance competition. Although very reluctant, Pat agrees to the compromise, and Tiffany promises to get Pat's letter to his wife. But as they practice together, something unexpected happens to Pat: dancing with Tiffany helps him stay focused and grounded. Ironically, Tiffany—a mysterious, depressed, and at times very outspoken woman—might just be the silver lining Pat is searching for.

## Discussion Questions

1. How would you describe Pat's communication competence? What about Tiffany's? In several scenes, the characters argue that the other one is "crazier" or "says more inappropriate things" than the other. Who is right?

2. Choose one of the characters in the film (Pat, Tiffany, Pat Sr., Dolores, or Ronnie) and analyze their approach to conflict. Which conflict style does this character use most often? How effective is their conflict style?

3. Describe the Solitano family's communication patterns (this includes Pat, Pat Sr., Dolores, and Jake). How is this family a system? Are they interdependent? What are their interaction patterns?

# SMOKE SIGNALS

## Film Data

| Year | 1998 |
|---|---|
| Director | Chris Eyre |
| Length | 89 minutes |
| Rating | PG-13 |

## Main Cast

| Character | Actor |
|---|---|
| Victor Joseph | Adam Beach |
| Thomas Builds-the-Fire | Evan Adams |
| Suzy Song | Irene Bedard |
| Arnold Joseph | Gary Farmer |
| Arlene Joseph | Tantoo Cardinal |
| Cathy | Cynthia Geary |
| Lucy | Elaine Miles |
| Velma | Michelle St. John |

## Communication Concepts

Narrative and Oral Tradition
Identity
Stereotypes
Conflict

## Viewing Information

Based on Alexie Sherman's book *The Lone Ranger and Tonto Fistfight in Heaven*, *Smoke Signals* broke new cinematic ground in 1998 as the first film to employ a Native director, screenwriter, producers, actors, and technicians. Acclaimed by critics and audiences alike, this road-trip movie boasts specific and broad appeal. A story about Native Americans rendered from a uniquely Native American perspective, it also explores universal themes of conflict, friendship, and family.

Of particular interest from a communication perspective are the constructs of identity and stereotypes, and the impact of narrative on self-concept, particularly within the oral tradition.

## Synopsis

After receiving news of his father's death in Arizona, Victor Joseph reluctantly allows Thomas Builds-the-Fire to finance a road trip to retrieve his ashes. Thomas has a condition, however: he gets to accompany Victor on the excursion. Fatefully intertwined lives on the C'oeur d'Alene reservation have not over the years generated a genuine friendship for cool Victor and nerdy Thomas, a relationship that Thomas has always desired. Opposites in almost every conceivable way, Victor, the strong, silent type, has unresolved anger issues stemming from his father's abandonment of their family. His interpersonal style in relationships is consequently as guarded, cynical, and taciturn as his would-be friend's is open, warm, and loquacious. Yet as their physical journey becomes a spiritual one, Victor learns to take different perspectives, feel empathy, and forgive himself and others.

## Discussion Questions
1. Discuss the importance of narrative for Thomas and Victor in their sense of cultural and personal identity. How do they see themselves within their narrative cultural tradition?
2. Discuss the treatment of stereotypes in this film.
3. Describe the principal interpersonal conflict in the story. How is it resolved?

# *SPANGLISH*

| Film Data | |
|---|---|
| Year | 2004 |
| Director | James L. Brooks |
| Length | 131 minutes |
| Rating | PG-13 |

| Main Cast | |
|---|---|
| Character | Actor |
| John Clasky | Adam Sandler |
| Deborah Clasky | Téa Leoni |
| Flor Moreno | Paz Vega |
| Evelyn Wright | Cloris Leachman |
| Cristina Moreno | Shelbie Bruce |
| Bernie Clasky | Sarah Steele |
| Georgie Clasky | Ian Hyland |

## Communication Concepts

Control and Power in Relationships
Defensive and Supportive Behaviors
Intercultural Communication
Relational Dialectics
Self-Concept and Identity Management

## Viewing Information

This drama-comedy profiles a family with quite different spouses. John Clasky is a devoted and thoughtful father. John's wife, Deborah, is divisive and condescending. When the radiant Spanish-speaking Flor takes the job of family housekeeper, what follows is a lesson not only in intercultural communication but family values as well.

*Synopsis*

*Spanglish* opens with a scene at the Admissions office of Princeton University. In a voice-over, we learn that applicant Cristina Moreno identifies "the most influential person in her life" as her mother—Flor Moreno. What unfolds is a story about Flor's decision to work for an Anglo family, the Claskys, and how her choice changes their lives forever.

The Clasky family consists of father John, mother Deborah, their two children Bernie and Georgie, and Deborah's mother Evelyn Wright. Flor quickly discovers that John is a highly successful, and perhaps overly emotional, chef; Deborah is neurotic and hyper-competitive, lifting herself up by putting others down; Evelyn is an alcoholic, though kind and generous; and the children are desperate for the positive influence missing from their mother. When Flor and Cristina are forced to move in with the Claskys during the summer, Flor loses all sense of privacy and is on the verge of quitting the job. By the film's end, it's up to Flor to make decisions that at least provide a chance of the Claskys rebuilding their lives.

*Discussion Questions*
1. Identify and contrast examples of Gibb's categories for defensive and supportive behaviors displayed by the characters. What effects do these behaviors have on their relationships?
2. Identify examples of one-up and one-down messages. Which relationships are complementary? Which are symmetrical?
3. Which dialectical tensions do John and Flor experience, both with each other and independently? How do they choose to manage these tensions?
4. How do the characters influence each other's self-concept? What influence does culture have on this process?

# *SPOTLIGHT*

| Film Data | |
|---|---|
| Year | 2015 |
| Director | Tom McCarthy |
| Length | 128 minutes |
| Rating | R |

| Main Cast | |
|---|---|
| **Character** | **Actor** |
| Mike Rezendes | Mark Ruffalo |
| Walter "Robby" Robinson | Michael Keaton |
| Sacha Pfeiffer | Rachel McAdams |
| Marty Baron | Liev Schreiber |
| Ben Bradlee Jr. | John Slattery |
| Mitchell Garabedian | Stanley Tucci |
| Jim Sullivan | Jamey Sheridan |
| Eric MacLeish | Billy Crudup |
| Phil Saviano | Neal Huff |
| Peter Conley | Paul Guilfoyle |
| Richard Sipe | Richard Jenkins |

## *Communication Concepts*

Agenda Setting and Media Framing
Facework and Identity Management
In-group–Out-group Bias
Small-Group Communication
Critical Thinking and Problem Solving

## Viewing Information

The winner of the Academy Award for Best Picture in 2016, this biopic depicts an exceptional year of actual investigative reporting, in-depth coverage of a massive scandal that had been covered up for decades. The work of the Spotlight team garnered the *Boston Globe* a Pulitzer Prize in 2003 for its revelations of sexual abuse and cover-up within the Boston Catholic Archdiocese, an exposé of tremendous local, national, and international significance. Accordingly, this film provides a compelling illustration of best practices in journalism and the effects of mass communication through media framing and agenda setting. It also reveals how a small group, one that excels at critical thinking and problem solving, can successfully tackle pervasive and entrenched institutional corruption.

## Synopsis

Based on a true story for which the *Boston Globe* received a Pulitzer Prize in 2003, *Spotlight* follows the investigative reporting team of the same name after their new editor at the *Boston Globe* assigns them the challenging task of exploring allegations of sexual abuse against Catholic priests in the Boston area. The journalists encounter pervasive and palpable resistance in their pursuit of a story critical of the Church, a historical pillar of tight-knit Boston communities. Dogged, diligent research of archived documents and countless interviews to follow up leads eventually reveal a scandal of epic proportions—abuse dating back decades and involving more priests and victims than the team could have ever initially imagined. Moreover, cover-up of the abuse was found to be equally extensive, extending to the highest levels of the archdiocese. The quake caused by Spotlight's groundbreaking and comprehensive coverage set off a tsunami of similar investigations that exposed systemic and worldwide abuse in the Catholic Church.

## Discussion Questions
1. How does the *Boston Globe*'s coverage of this scandal demonstrate agenda setting and framing, two theories that are often invoked in investigations of media effects?
2. Describe the facework and identity management of the central figures involved in the story uncovered by the Spotlight team?
3. Discuss the importance of in-groups and out-groups in Boston. How does in-group–out-group bias affect the interaction between the characters and the development of the story?
4. Explain how critical thinking shapes the small-group problem-solving approach of the journalists featured in Spotlight?

# STRAIGHT OUTTA COMPTON

## Film Data

| Year | 2015 |
|------|------|
| Director | F. Gary Gray |
| Length | 147 minutes |
| Rating | R |

## Main Cast

| Character | Actor |
|-----------|-------|
| Ice Cube | O'Shea Jackson Jr. |
| Dr. Dre | Corey Hawkins |
| Eazy-E | Jason Mitchell |
| DJ Yella | Neil Brown Jr. |
| MC Ren | Aldis Hodge |
| D.O.C. | Marlon Yates Jr. |
| Jerry Heller | Paul Giamatti |

## Communication Concepts

Small-Group and Team Communication
Conflict
Cocultural Communication

## Viewing Information

*Straight Outta Compton* is an acclaimed 2015 biopic, a commercial and critical success that remains rather controversial nonetheless for the negative story or stories that it didn't tell. Gangsta rap pioneers N.W.A. have been censured for lyrics that some argue promote misogyny and violence against certain groups, notably the police. Dr. Dre's history from this era also includes episodes of physical assault against women, not addressed or even suggested in the film. These are important omissions to consider in addition to what we do see, a story that offers material rich in the subject areas of conflict, teamwork, and artistic expression.

## *Synopsis*

*Straight Outta Compton* depicts the rise of gangsta rap group N.W.A. from Compton, a city plagued in the 1980s by not only gang violence but also policing of gang violence experienced by the black community and immortalized in N.W.A lyrics as harassment and brutality. Its five original members—Eazy-E, Ice Cube, Dr. Dre, DJ Yella, and MC Ren—emerge as a West Coast supergroup notorious for controversial rhymes that exposed the realities of life in the hood, where conflict of every stripe is the norm. Chief among these conflicts were clashes between young black men like N.W.A. and the local police, hostile and often violent encounters described and, some argued, exacerbated by N.W.A.'s candid, unapologetic, and aggressively edgy lyrics, and their musical protest of mistreatment by the authorities. They managed to creatively channel this external conflict into hit music but were less adept at addressing internal conflict within the group. These tensions eventually led to their breakup, with Ice Cube and Dr. Dre leaving to pursue successful solo careers.

## *Discussion Questions*

1. Is N.W.A. a rap group that also qualifies as a team? What are the characteristics of a team, and how does N.W.A function, or fail to function, in these ways?
2. Describe some of the numerous instances of conflict in the film and the different approaches to conflict resolution. What role does conflict play in N.W.A.'s rise to stardom on both creative and commercial levels?
3. At what points does N.W.A. equate their work with that of journalists? Do you support this comparison, and what are its implications? Should the protection of free speech also apply to violent or misogynistic lyrics, two criticisms levied at rap music in general and N.W.A.'s lyrics in particular?

# THE THEORY OF EVERYTHING

*Film Data*

| Year | 2014 |
|---|---|
| Director | James Marsh |
| Length | 123 minutes |
| Rating | PG-13 |

*Main Cast*

| Character | Actor |
|---|---|
| Stephen Hawking | Eddie Redmayne |
| Jane Hawking | Felicity Jones |
| Jonathan Jones | Charlie Cox |
| Dennis Sciama | David Thewlis |

*Communication Concepts*

Intimacy
Identity/Self- Concept
Nonverbal Communication
Relational Development

*Viewing Information*

*The Theory of Everything* is an award-winning film adaptation of Jane Hawking's biography, focusing on the relationship between her and her famous physicist husband, Stephen Hawking. The film concentrates on the relationship between the two likable characters from their initial meeting at Oxford through Stephen's diagnosis with ALS and the progression of the disease. While the film does touch on some of Stephen Hawking's scientific work, it is not by any means a technically oriented film. The film is rated PG-13 for some language and adult themes.

*Synopsis*

Stephen Hawking was a young doctoral student studying physics at Cambridge in the 1960s when he met and fell in love with Jane. Not long after beginning their relationship, Stephen was diagnosed with ALS and given two years to live. Jane refused to give up on the relationship, and became not only Stephen's wife, but the mother of his three children and his caretaker as his physical situation declined. As shown in the film the two begin to drift apart, and end up divorcing after more than 20 years together.

*Discussion Questions*
1.  We get to witness Stephen and Jane's relationship from initial encounter to dissolution of their marriage. Identify the key moments of Knapp's relational stages shown in the movie. What did they do (or not do) that allowed their relationship to progress to the next stages?
2.  Jane's sense of identity appears to evolve over the time covered by the movie, from a poetry student to a young wife and mother, to a full-time nurse and caretaker, even handling Stephen's business affairs. Identify the points where Jane noticed the changes. How did she deal with them?
3.  What types of intimacy were demonstrated throughout the film? How did the types of intimacy vary based on the relationships? How is intimacy a factor in the building or coming apart of relationships?

# UP IN THE AIR

| Film Data | |
|---|---|
| Year | 2009 |
| Director | Jason Reitman |
| Length | 108 minutes |
| Rating | R |

| Main Cast | |
|---|---|
| Character | Actor |
| Ryan Bingham | George Clooney |
| Alex Goran | Vera Farmiga |
| Natalie Keener | Anna Kendrick |
| Craig Gregory | Jason Bateman |
| Bob | J.K. Simmons |
| Jim Miller | Danny McBride |

*Communication Concepts*

Computer-Mediated Communication
Perspective Taking and Person-Centered Messages
Relational Commitment/Dialectics

*Viewing Information*

Ryan Bingham is a corporate downsizer who flies around the country firing people and avoiding relationships. Enter Natalie Keener, a feisty college graduate who wants to upend Ryan's business, and Alex Goran, an attractive business traveler who captures Ryan's heart. The results are a funny, ironic take on both romantic relationships and corporate culture. And as the title suggests, both women may indeed leave Ryan "up in the air."

*Synopsis*

Ryan Bingham is an island surrounded by a sea of travelers. Working for a company that specializes in corporate downsizing, Ryan is paid, essentially, to fire people. And apparently he is very good at what he does: Ryan's company flies him around the country over 300 days out of the year. He also gives motivational speeches about "relational downsizing" and about living one's life out of a backpack—a metaphor for Ryan's lifestyle. Clearly more at home on the road, Ryan's way of life is threatened when the company hires Natalie Keener, an overly ambitious college graduate who wants to revolutionize his business: Natalie believes that employees can be fired through teleconferencing and not in person. If that weren't threatening enough, Ryan begins a romantic relationship with fellow business traveler Alex, who causes him to question his self-imposed isolationism. Ryan Bingham might be an island, but he soon realizes that he is not alone.

*Discussion Questions*
1. Compare and contrast Natalie, Alex, and Ryan and their divergent views on relational commitment. How do all the characters define their romantic relationships? How do they manage the autonomy versus connection relational dialectic?
2. Analyze examples of person-centered messages Ryan creates as part of his job, and compare those with the messages he creates while not working. In which context is he more skilled at perspective taking? In which context is he more scripted?
3. Identify examples of computer-mediated communication (CMC) used throughout the film. In the business context, how effective is CMC? How do the characters use CMC outside of work?

# SECTION IV
# FEATURE FILM WEBSITES OF INTEREST

The Internet Movie Database
www.imdb.com

MTV News: Movies
www.film.com

Metacritic
http://www.metacritic.com

Rotten Tomatoes
https://www.rottentomatoes.com

Slant
http://www.slantmagazine.com

The Film Stage: Your Spotlight on Cinema
https://thefilmstage.com

Fandor
https://www.fandor.com/keyframe/

Movie Review Query Engine
www.mrqe.com

Roger Ebert Reviews
rogerebert.suntimes.com

Film Clips Online
www.filmclipsonline.com

# INDEX BY COMMUNICATION CONCEPTS